Warm Hearts
and Cold Cash

Warm Hearts and Cold Cash

The Intimate Dynamics of Families and Money

MARCIA MILLMAN

THE FREE PRESS
A Division of Macmillan, Inc.
NEW YORK

Collier Macmillan Canada
TORONTO

Maxwell Macmillan International
NEW YORK   OXFORD   SINGAPORE   SYDNEY

The Free Press
A Division of Macmillan, Inc.
866 Third Avenue, New York, N.Y. 10022

Collier Macmillan Canada, Inc.
1200 Eglinton Avenue East
Suite 200
Don Mills, Ontario M3C 3N1

Printed in the United States of America

printing number
1 2 3 4 5 6 7 8 9 10

Library of Congress Cataloging-in-Publication Data

Millman, Marcia.
   Warm hearts and cold cash : the intimate dynamics of families and money / Marcia Millman.
      p. cm.
   ISBN 0-02-921285-5
   1. Family—Economic aspects—United States. 2. Finance, Personal —United States. I. Title.
HQ536.M54   1991
306.85'0973—dc20   90-25094
                                                                    CIP

CREDITS

Brief quotations reprinted from *Liar's Poker: Rising Through the Wreckage on Wall Street*, by Michael Lewis, by permission of the author and W. W. Norton & Company, Inc. Copyright © 1989 by Michael Lewis.
Excerpt from *A Room of One's Own* by Virginia Woolf, copyright 1929 by Harcourt Brace Jovanovich, Inc. and renewed 1957 by Leonard Woolf, reprinted by permission of the publisher.

*To Arthur and Shirley Schrager
and to Carol Hill*

Contents

Preface

*P*opular culture and the social sciences all share a tendency to take family love as a given, as nonproblematic. But it seems to me that in real life, people are much less certain about love. Does he or she *really* love me? *How much* does he or she love me? are the persistent, disturbing questions that often dominate our relationships with partners, parents, children, and siblings. Children continually question whether their parents truly love them, and later in life, parents often feel unloved because their children seem neglectful or indifferent. Despite our images of the family as the place where people feel secure in love, in real life, love is more ambiguous, unequal, unsteady, and uncertain.

As a sociologist, I've also been puzzled at the fact that my profession largely ignores the competitive aspects of family life. We view the family as a warm haven from the cold, hard world outside, but in many ways, families are infused with rivalry. Furthermore, we are bound to our families not just through love, but also through dependence and guilt. I wanted to examine these aspects of family life that get left out of our sentimentalized portraits, and it seemed to me that family money would provide the most revealing window.

In the context of rivalry and uncertainty about love, money takes on a special significance. Since love is ambiguous and unmeasurable, we look for something clear and quantifiable to gauge and judge feelings and relationships. Money also becomes an equivalent for love and often serves as a payment or substitute for attention and affection.

To explore this subject, I interviewed many people—both

strangers and acquaintances—about the roles money had played in their relationships, and discussed the subject endlessly with my friends. I also spent several months in courthouses, observing cases in which relatives were suing one another over contested wills and divorces. It's not always clear whether people are fighting over love or money, or for that matter, whether they stay attached because of love or money. In the end, love and money become so mixed up that people are frequently confused about their own motives and desires. My reflections on the stories and cases I encountered are my effort to untangle these two powerful forces that form the major preoccupations of our lives.

Acknowledgments

I would like to express my appreciation to several institutions for making this work possible: to the University of California at Santa Cruz, which for many years has given me the support and freedom to follow my research interests wherever they have led, and to Blue Mountain Lake, MacDowell, and Yaddo, for allowing me to be their guest and treating me with such kindness.

I am grateful for the intellectual stimulation and personal encouragement I received from friends and colleagues. I especially want to thank Naomi Bushman, Carol Hill, John Kitsuse, Marty Klein, B. K. Moran, and Barrie Thorne. Also, Nancy Adler, Monty Amyx, Alexandra Botwin, Arlene Daniels, Liz Darhansoff, Edith Lewis, Peter Lyman, Melanie Mayer, Jerry Platt, and Dora Ullian. I want to express my deep appreciation to my editor, Peter Dougherty, for his astute suggestions and thoughtful criticisms, and his unfailing patience and support.

Finally, I want to express my gratitude to the people who appear in this book, though I have not used their real names. I thank them for allowing me to interview them, and for opening their lives and thoughts to me, and for giving this book its life.

1

———•———

Love and Money

*I*t's ironic that in the world of commerce we have elaborate laws
and contracts for insuring some protection and fairness in our
financial dealings with one another, but to those we love the most,
we offer no such guarantees. Our image of the family as a warm,
cozy place where people can trust one another prevents us from
thinking that any rules, discussion, or even reflection about money
are required. We're willing to risk our futures on blind faith that
blood is thicker than water. In many families and intimate relationships, just bringing up the subject of money is taken as an ugly
sign of lack of trust. Our assumption of this trust even prevents us
from examining how money operates in families, or from considering the consequences of different financial arrangements.

Of course, anyone who has been cheated or burned begins
wondering about the basis of that trust. By now, we know a lot
about the financial injustices associated with divorce, but we don't
often examine the broader subject of how money is shared, divided, and used in families, and with what consequences.

Our society provides few explicit conventions or guidelines for
dealing with family money, so many people wind up feeling
cheated. We don't have to go through an ugly divorce or lose an
inheritance we expected to discover that financial arrangements
among relatives can be hurtful and unjust. But even if we lack
explicit rules about family money, we still have deep expectations,
and when these expectations are disappointed, people are devastated.

In other times and places, there have been clear understandings
and rules for dowries, bride prices, primogeniture, the transfer

1

of property from one generation to the next. These arrangements are not left to chance or to the judgment of individual families, because it's understood that the structure of the society is tied to the ways that financial dealings are regulated within families. In our own society, upper-class WASP families have a broadly shared culture governing family money that is designed to safeguard their social and economic position—with rules such as not spoiling children by giving them too much when they're young, or preserving the family's wealth for the next generation by spending only the interest and never the principal of inherited money.

In the American middle class, however, there is much less of an identifiable canon for dealing with family money. We accept the constraints and intrusions of social norms, proprieties, and moral judgments in many other areas of life, but we wouldn't think of intruding on the privacy of families when it comes to dealing with money. Aside from state laws that specify how marital property is defined and divided upon divorce, and laws that specify how money is to be distributed if a person dies without a will, we back off from any legal or cultural guidance about dealing with money in the family. Perhaps the one principle widely accepted in the middle class is that children should be given equal amounts. Even this principle is difficult to apply, however, given the fact that different children present unequal needs, talents, desires, and capacities. Still, the principle's moral weight is revealed by the guilt that many parents express when they privately acknowledge how unequally they've treated their children.

Perhaps the middle class hasn't felt a need for a social code relating to family money because not much has seemed to be at stake. Until recently, only a small fraction of American families had any substantial fortune to pass on to the next generation. The middle or lower-middle classes focused more on economic and social mobility than on what one might inherit.

Because the middle class emphasizes individual mobility and personal autonomy above all else, it has few shared values and customs concerned with money in the family. When money is earned rather than inherited, when identity is based on individual achievement rather than membership in a family, there is little need to impose collective rules and norms on family finances.

For most of this century, the primary legacy of middle-class parents to children has been "cultural" capital—the upbringing and education that allowed children to become financially successful and independent of their parents. In earlier times, when family inheritances consisted of land or a business, children had to wait for their parents to die before they could be independent. And since land and businesses can't always be usefully divided, the inheritance was often restricted to one child, usually the oldest son.

In contrast, cultural capital enabled middle-class parents to give all of their children a good start in life. Siblings were not direct competitors, because as long as there was enough money to raise and educate all of them, what was given to one in no way diminished what was given to another. Furthermore, cultural capital freed children from parental control because, once it was given, it could not be taken back.

This situation is rapidly changing because the generation of middle-class Americans that started rearing families after World War II (parents now in their fifties to seventies) have amassed a huge amount of money in the value of their homes and stocks that they are passing on to the baby-boom generation through inheritances and gifts—money that is enormously consequential in shaping the lives of their adult children.

According to several estimates and reports[1] there will be an immense transfer of wealth—$7 to $8 trillion—from parents to children in the next twenty years. Until recently it was assumed (among all but the very wealthy) that once children were out of college, parents stopped supporting them. Today, American adults in their twenties, thirties, and forties are financially dependent on aging parents for graduate degrees, down payments for houses, start-up money for businesses, college tuition for their children, and even living expenses if they've been impoverished by divorce.

What distinguishes the current generation of middle-class adult baby boomers is that a large percentage of them will be receiving substantial sums from their parents. While much of this wealth is concentrated among the most affluent, it's been estimated that one in ten baby boomers will receive an inheritance of at least $400,000 and one in three will inherit enough to pay cash for a house.[2] Furthermore, the circumstances of life (such as the cost of housing) have changed to make baby boomers seriously dependent on those sums. My research indicates that in many families, this is causing considerable conflict and distress because parents and their children don't know and often disagree about what is owed to adult children, or the best way to make these gifts, or how to divide this wealth among children with different needs. The new significance of middle-class wealth gives us one more reason to examine how money operates in families, as well as the consequences of different financial arrangements.

This book explores how money seeps into love and intimate relationships, and the troubles that ensue when people can't untangle the web of love and money. Many of us have difficulty dealing with a combination of the two, because we've been taught that money is irrelevant to love. But any close relationship, whether between parents and children, married or unmarried couples, friends, siblings, or business partners, will eventually be affected by money.

Dealing with money in the context of love or family is extremely difficult because it involves a compound problem that requires us to separate financial decisions from emotional ones, while recognizing and handling both kinds. It's hard to deal with these problems because money often calls attention to aspects of a relationship that people would rather not face or talk about. Indeed, we seem to have a remarkable capacity for lying to ourselves about our closest relationships, and our illusions are often shattered only by the indisputable figures of money. But when we choose not to acknowledge the roles and powers of money in a relationship, or to control them, we pay the price of having money control us instead.

It's foolish to pretend that money is irrelevant to love. In a market economy, money is not only power but also the ultimate measure of value; for this reason, it insinuates itself into even the most intimate settings. And money is so plastic it can turn itself into anything. As both Shakespeare and Marx have observed, an ugly man with money can buy himself a beautiful woman and therefore not suffer the consequences of being ugly. For all intents and purposes, he is not ugly—money gives him a different face. Money, being the ultimate measure of value, winds up creating reality.

In a mobile society, like our own, we believe that identity is not conferred by who our parents are or where we come from, rather identity is viewed as self-created. Without another source of identification, money not only is the ultimate measure of worth, but often becomes the primary determinant of identity. It takes the place of all the other traditional badges. A friend of mine who is a financial advisor charges his clients $350 per hour for his services, and he has more business than he can handle. He smiles at the thought that people will pay that much for his time. His pleasure in his earnings derives more from that measure of his value than the objects his money can buy. Conversely, the person who can't find a job, or only one that pays the minimum wage, has to work hard at not feeling worthless.

Money is a primary source of power in relationships, too; without it, we are dependent. Having money allows us to control other people or be free of them, even rid of them, as it allows the other to be free of us. Attorneys like to say that it's the person who wants to get out of a relationship who has to pay. Money is a powerful adhesive. Were it not for the financial consequences, even more of us would be leaving our spouses or business partners. When you don't have enough money to buy your freedom or to pay your partner to disappear, you have to make the best of things. Even those who are beyond trying to get along with a partner may still be stuck. As a recent cover story in *New York* magazine illustrated, today there are nightmarish "live-in divorces" because in expensive cities even affluent couples who are no longer communicating except through their lawyers may have to share a home for a few years or adjust to living in a studio apartment.[3]

Money also defines us because we express ourselves in what we buy. When market researchers investigate our spending habits, they're not just assessing the relationship between income and expenditures—they're seeking the connection between self-image and what people will spend their money on. We have a way of pouring ourselves into our possessions. We don't just own them— they own us. They become a part of us, especially the possessions we feel most identified with, like houses, cars, and pets.

We express ourselves not just in the objects we buy but in every financial move we make. When we talk about the "bottom line" and "putting your money where your mouth is," we understand that money tells the truth like nothing else. Spending money is not just a measure of commitment, it's a measure of feeling. A friend of mine recalled how at the passionate start of a relationship, her long-distance lover was always willing to spend whatever it cost to be with her—even several hundred dollars for a long weekend together. Toward the end of the relationship, when his feelings cooled, he started watching pennies. Though she tried to reassure herself that he was merely reverting to his more customary frugality and a lifelong effort to impersonate a Boston Brahmin, she knew he no longer loved her when she arrived for a visit and they went shopping for the weekend's groceries. When she saw him tossing half-priced, outdated sirloin into the basket and picking up a thin package of turkey breast slices to use in lieu of veal for the scallopini, she knew it was time to pack her bags. She had to fight back tears at the realization that she'd just spent *her* last savings and traveled three thousand miles to visit a wealthy man who would feed her rotten meat.

Even in marriage, the willingness to spend money is a sign of commitment or the price one pays to keep the love alive. A man I know who hates to spend money on travel gives in to his wife's enthusiasm for trips and hotels because he knows he has to spend that money to keep her happy and the relationship intact. Everyone jokes about couples who renovate their houses just before they divorce, but it's not the upheaval of construction that causes people to part but rather the prior tensions that caused them to make one last show of solidarity by investing money in their home.

In families, as well as courtship, a present is often taken as a sign of feeling or even of character. A friend of mine described a birthday present she'd received from her selfish mother-in-law: a dress her mother-in-law had originally sewn for herself but had found unflattering. When my friend asked her mother-in-law why she hadn't given the dress to her own daughter, the answer was, "Oh, Barbara would never wear this dress, she likes *sexy* clothes."

We joke about it, but in the family, as in the marketplace, money is often the measure of every reality, including love. And because money is so definite, precise, and measurable, it cuts through the illusions and habituated blindnesses of love with clarity.

At a dinner party a few years ago, I heard a story of family money I will never forget. Albert was about sixty. When his father had died the year before, he'd shocked everyone with his will. Albert's father had left $20,000 to each of his grandchildren, except for the two offspring of his deceased son (Albert's late brother, John) with whom he'd not been on speaking terms during the last few years before John died. John's children, though most in need of money, were left only a small fraction of the sum given to their cousins. Apparently, their father's guilt was to be carried over to the next generation.

An even greater shock was in store for Albert, always the closest to the father among the three siblings. The bulk of the estate was divided evenly between Albert and his surviving sibling, a sister, but with the following provision: Albert's sister was given her half-million dollars free and clear, but Albert can touch only the interest—not the principal—of his inheritance until the day his wife dies. If his wife, Carolyn, outlives Albert (which is probable, since she's fifteen years younger), the money will eventually pass to their children, except they, too, cannot have it until their mother is dead. Even a divorce will not break the curse—the money is untouchable until the wicked witch is dead.

By now, everyone at the dinner table had stopped eating, and Carolyn (who is charming and lovely) told us that until her father-in-law died she had no idea that he hated her so much. Albert added that although he'd always worshipped his father, he now recognized him as a spiteful man who'd planned this punishment for the pleasure of knowing he'd control Albert's family for the next forty years.

It turns out that Albert, who had always lived near his father in New York, moved to Washington, D.C., a few years before, because his wife's career required it. After his mother died, Albert dutifully visited his father in New York every two weeks, but I imagine this wasn't enough for the old man. Every time Albert departed for Washington, his father must have burned with indignation at being deserted because of this woman.

With his will Albert's father achieved the perfect revenge. The old man was forced to share his son with his daughter-in-law, but he didn't have to share his money with her. Now his daughter-in-law would find out, as he had, what it's like to have children who can't wait for you to die.

There is also a rationale of sorts to the old man's unequal treatment of the grandchildren. If his deceased, oldest son had been a good child, he would have repaid the kindness by providing for the son's offspring. But since the son was a disappointment, in the grandfather's system of accounting, nothing was owed to these grandchildren.

In addition to the hostility they expressed, the terms of the will have also succeeded in dividing Albert and his sister. Recently, Albert's business was in difficulties. Needing cash to save it, he complained to his sister about the will, hoping she'd get the hint and offer to share some of her money. "What's so terrible about living off the interest?" she replied, and the conversation was over.

For Albert, the will revealed the true, mean character of his father, but to me, it reveals something more universal about family life. In families there is a constant activity of accounting, both emotional and financial, with deep expectations and definite, if unspoken, rules of exchange. Though we commonly romanticize the family as the one place where all is shared and where nobody measures, in fact there is probably more counting in families than in any other close circle. What may start as a grievance over attention or love that was desired and not received is often converted into a financial debit. Money, perfectly plastic, so capable of converting itself into any substance or form, seeps so deeply into the realm of feeling that it becomes an equivalent and is always available as a substitute.

A little history lends perspective. The common, if misguided, notion of the family as a haven from the cold and uncaring world of the marketplace is a relatively recent invention. This conception of the family fully took hold in European and North American societies only in the nineteenth century, as industrialization progressively separated the life of the family from the life of the workplace. As the workplace became more impersonal, the family was increasingly regarded as the loving and accepting refuge from the hard world outside.

The two worlds were split in popular culture as well as social science, and they largely remain so. Although the romantic image of the family has been tarnished a little by the realities of divorce, we still assume that relationships in the family work according to different principles from those in the marketplace. The public world is still seen as an unfeeling market revolving around money, where contracts are needed to regulate relationships that are competitive and largely impersonal. In contrast, the family is viewed as a refuge of permanent attachment, unconditional sharing, and mutual aid, driven and consolidated by love rather than by money.

In fact, the family is a lot more complex than that. In many ways, families display the same hard traits of the market. One sees this expressed in the ways we use money, often unconsciously, to control children, punish estranged spouses, measure a parent's true feelings for us, buy freedom from relationships, or stop a partner from leaving. Furthermore, in the family, as in the workplace, there is a system of exchange with perpetual accounting and sanctions for not performing as expected. But because of our image of the family as a place of love and sharing (and our deep wish that it be so) we underestimate the conflicts of interest and rivalries that are common, if not inevitable, and make light of the deadly serious bookkeeping.

What is the accounting system of the family? In his discussion of different kinds of economies, Kenneth Boulding[4] distinguishes the exchange economy of the marketplace from the "reciprocity" of the family. According to Boulding, exchange is conditional ("I will give you so much of x if you give me so much of y") and is based on the acceptance of a conditional offer. In contrast, Boulding argues, the reciprocity of the family is formally unconditional and more like a set of grants: thus, A gives something to B out of her feeling for B, and B gives something to A out of his feeling for A, but the two acts are not formally related since neither is a condition of the other.

That is how we idealize the family, and yet we should know better. Even Boulding admits that the reciprocity of the family often edges into an economy of exchange: "Christmas presents are a good example of an activity that frequently involves reciprocity and occasionally degenerates into exchange."[5]

In my view, the reciprocity of the family is a lot less voluntary than we like to recognize. Not only do family members count money, they tally all measures of feeling, and soon money and feeling become intertwined in the balance sheet. "Freely" given presents are remembered by the donor as much as by the recipient, even more so. When a relative doesn't display a feeling that another believes is owed, old gifts are recalled as evidence of the debt.

A friend of mine observed that when her relatives gossip about each other, money always comes up when a family member has misbehaved. She remembered that after her father had a heart attack, her family was offended that one of her "close" cousins never called to ask how his uncle was. Complaining about this cousin, they recalled that when he'd last been treated to dinner at the country club by her father, this ungrateful cousin had upgraded his meal (and its cost) by ordering both shrimp as an appetizer and lobster as the main course.

The stories in this book explore this intricate economy of love and money in the family; it examines relationships that are supposed to be voluntary and reciprocal but gravitate toward conditional exchange. The stories also reveal a good deal about people's notions of justice and injustice concerning family money. Although we don't have many clear rules, people know when they've been wronged.

To learn about this family economy and these notions of financial justice, I interviewed people who have lived through interesting experiences with love and money, the kinds of experiences that usually make us more self-reflective. They include people who have moved from one social class to another; people who received a windfall, like a million-dollar lottery prize; people who have divorced; and people who have made, lost, married, and inherited fortunes. In addition I interviewed people who are professional experts in the realms of love and money: accountants, financial advisors, and attorneys who specialize in estate planning and divorce. Finally, I spent several months in court, observing trials that involved contested wills and divorces, remarkable occasions for witnessing the convergence of love and money. During these trials, I came to know several of the adversaries well, taking advantage of the intensity of the occasion and the long court recesses and delays to hear their reactions to the unfolding dramas. All names have been changed to protect the privacy of my informants and subjects.

Facing a parent or a former spouse in court, and going head to head with them about what was given and what was owed, is truly an astonishing ordeal. What with witnesses, cross-examination, and damaging documents, one can't help but wonder what would make a person do this. I admit to shock at the betrayals of intimacy I've seen used as evidence: love letters written in happier times, diaries never meant to be seen by another living soul, documents pointing to financial manipulations and tax evasion that could send someone to jail. Perhaps people who would go this far in revealing themselves and someone they once loved belong to a separate breed, but I don't really think so. They're just more willing than most to expose their private lives in order to get what they think is coming to them. I found that divorce, especially, provides a rich opportunity to study people who are dealing with the convergence of love and money.

Only upon divorcing do many people confront the fact that

marriage and family life are organized around money as much as anything else. People go into marriage believing it's about love, but when love has vanished, there's only money left to divide and fight over. In retrospect, marriage seems to have been about money all along, but looking back at something that's gone also obscures the earlier experience. One friend of mine, who resented having to support a wife who had hurt and deserted him, put it this way:

> There are two structures to marriage, the structure of love and the financial contract. Love is ephemeral, but the financial contract you make with a spouse is not. When you get married, it's to that contract of financial obligation in perpetuity, not of love. You don't hear it in the marriage ceremony which only says you will love, honor, and obey. You only see it in bold relief when you get divorced, but it should be part of the marriage ceremony: it's more fundamental, and it's the basis of the relationship. Love is just the patina on what you really get into.

Not only does romanticized love obscure the underlying financial relationship of marriage, but when love evaporates, many discover that what had seemed like love at the time turns out to have been a kind of work all along. In court, one hears this all the time: "My husband was a full-time job," pleads one wife, justifying why she'd earned no money after they married. Another woman who appears in this book defends her decision to keep half of her husband's family inheritance, even though she's divorcing him because he's ended up in a mental hospital. For years she had lived with his depressions and toiled endlessly to prop him up. If it hadn't been for her, she claims, he'd never have sustained his relationship with his parents and collected his inheritance. As the stories show, the "love" that is reciprocally given in families is neither spontaneous nor free of charge. Those who "give support" experience it not only as love but as work, and those who do more of it expect to be compensated in cash when love has been exhausted.

There is another factor in the economy of love and money, and that's the tendency for people to repeat their parents' experiences or to relive childhood dramas in their adult lives. The reach of the past into the relations of the present seems almost universal. It's really not surprising, considering that our expectations about love are strongly influenced by our early experiences. Hoping to escape from the past, many people turn to money as the ticket out of hell, though often in vain.

I often think about a friend whose life and fortune peaked when he was only eleven years old. A celebrated whiz kid of the 1950s, he was already nationally known for his precocity when he decided, at the age of eleven, to make his family rich by winning on a television game show.

My friend's family (father, mother, younger sister) lived in the South, but to carry out his plan, my friend and his mother moved to New York for a few months and shared a room in a hotel near the public library on 42nd Street. In between shows, as he worked his way up toward the grand prize, my friend studied frantically in his hotel room while his mother carried books back and forth from the library. He did win the "grand prize" and later, even more on other shows.

My friend always insisted that going on television was all his own idea and that his parents hadn't exploited him. But he also told me that even as a child he'd known his mother was dissatisfied with his father's earnings. By the time my friend was eleven he'd made his family rich, but the success wasn't only monetary. More importantly, this small child had rescued his mother from the boredom and disappointment of her marriage.

I often think of the months he spent alone with his mother, cramming books and facts in the depressing hotel room, then marching each week on stage and into the show's gaudy "isolation booth." He was so small he could barely peer through the window, yet he always came up with the right answer, while the nation watched and held its breath. Surely this adventure was a most intoxicating and formative romance. It established a pitch of excitement he demanded of all later loves and achievements, and making money was forever linked with his search for love.

A story by D. H. Lawrence, "The Rocking Horse Winner," tells of a child who overhears his wasteful parents talking about their money woes. The child discovers a magical way to save them: by rocking on his toy horse and concentrating fiercely he was able to conjure up the name of the horse that would win at the next race. Using the family butler to place his bets, he manages to win money and sneak it into the family coffers. But his parents keep spending whatever the child wins, and he has to work harder and harder, until finally, one day, the child rocks himself into exhaustion and dies.

Many of the people who appear in this book are like the rocking-horse boy. As children, they observed what made their parents miserable, and their life has been a quest to mend that sorrow. As in the story of the rocking-horse boy, money is typically a magical substance in their tales, and so is it truly one in real life. Although many of the people I write about managed to escape the material poverty and social limitations of their parents' lives, they rarely escaped the disappointing emotional circumstances they'd experienced as children. It's often easier to flee from one's class origins than one's early experience of love.

Having said that money is revealing, that the family is more like a market than we like to think, and that people often get stuck in repetitive, unhappy scenarios, I would not go so far as to say that we are slaves to money and its role in our formative experiences, that we exercise no choice. Facing up to the realities, both emotional and financial, is a necessary condition for exercising choice, but the payoff is that we are then free to arrange our finances so they enrich our relationships rather than corrupt them. But to do this, we must be aware of the roles that money plays in our relationships with parents, partners, and children. Denying or ignoring the powers of money in the family does not make them vanish, it only leaves us more vulnerable to the considerable forces that money can unleash.

Lionel Trilling described how money can take over, invading spaces it wasn't supposed to reach: "Money is both real and not real, like a spook. We invented money and we use it, yet we cannot either understand its laws or control its actions. It has a life of its own which it properly should not have; Karl Marx speaks with a kind of horror of its indecent power to reproduce, as if, he says, love were working in its body."[6]

The belief that money inevitably corrupts relationships is almost universal among serious observers. This corrupting aspect of money is a general principle that most of us accept (even as we deny that it operates in our own relationships). And yet, it should also become clear that people can use money to advance their other goals rather than be money's passive victims. As the sociologist Viviana Zelizer illustrates in her examination of "special monies,"[7] people don't necessarily have to surrender to money, but can shape money and determine its meanings. Zelizer describes how we assign different meanings and designate special uses for various kinds of money. We tend to treat wages, inheritances, gifts, allowances, and domestic money in distinct ways. As Zelizer argues, all dollars are not equal. Pointing to the ways that societies and cultures differentiate special monies and restrict their uses, Zelizer challenges the assumption of Georg Simmel, Karl Marx, and other classical theorists that modern, "market money" turns all feelings, values, and objects into homogenized cash equivalents.

As the stories in this book illustrate, family money is viewed as a special kind of money, and it takes on many symbolic meanings beyond its actual cash value. This is true precisely because family money is so tangled up with love and our feelings about how well or badly we've been treated by those we love. It's also true, as Marx and Simmel argued, that money has real consequences, that money exerts its own powerful influence, and that money *does* transform relationships. Yet we need not throw up our hands and relinquish any control over either the real power or the symbolic meanings of family money. Dealing with family money is embarrassing and awkward because money challenges our romanticized views of the family, and talking about it exposes family grudges and envies, as well as the almost-universal (at least in our culture) feeling that one was not loved enough or given enough attention. But since family money is becoming increasingly important in our lives and relationships, it's time we faced up to it, both personally and collectively. Being explicit about money doesn't have to corrupt our relationships, it can enhance them.

Georg Simmel and others have argued that money exchanges are fitting only for the impersonal market, whereas presents meant for tribute must be personal. Many of us *are* uneasy about giving cash for a gift since cash is viewed as so antithetical to the principles that define relationships of love. Indeed, giving money often signals the end of a personal tie, while in an ongoing relationship one can run up a tab. As Simmel argued, when the client pays the prostitute, he frees himself from further obligation. On the other hand, as we've all discovered, nonmonetary gifts are frequently inefficient. Though they may be personally chosen for the recipient, they often miss the mark. People are more likely to wind up with what they want if they're given cash.

This is true for all kinds of money, not just gifts. As the stories in this book illustrate, we can deal with naked cash in a way that will control other people, or use it to give them independence. And just as money gifts may allow people to choose what they really want, so may we be more successful in getting what we want in relationships if we're willing to face up to the fact that love involves conditional exchanges and bargaining. When we face it, honestly and explicitly, money is a powerful tool that can serve our chosen values, but left unexamined, it tends, as Marx argued, to take on a life of its own.

Many of the stories that follow are about people who wound up financially and emotionally devastated because they couldn't acknowledge or deal with some disturbing truths about themselves, the people they loved, their relationships, or the nature of family life itself. Their levels of insight into their situations vary widely, but all of them offer lessons we can use. Their experiences also point to the consequences that follow from different kinds of financial decisions. Because my focus is on the problems that money presents, the stories emphasize the more disturbing aspects of family life. Of course, families are also the settings for great generosity, but we don't need another sentimental portrait.

In the end, money doesn't corrupt love or families so much as it illuminates them. As the stain on furniture shows the deep grain of the wood, so does money reveal the hidden structures and rules of family life. This is why people have so much trouble with it: money always threatens to uncover what families go to such trouble to disguise. After listening to people talk about love and money, I'm convinced that in every life there are times when money throws a brilliant light on the shadowy worlds that we each come to know as love and family. The stories that follow are about these large and small moments of truth.

2

—•—

Rude Awakenings

*I*n her memoir of growing up after World War I in a poor Jewish immigrant family, the writer Kate Simon recalls her father in a brilliant anecdote involving money. As children, she and her brother were constantly warned by their mother to be quiet when their irritable father came home from work because he would be "nervous" from the day's labors and frustrations. At dinner, her father unfailingly complained about the shoes his children ruined so quickly, the butter they smeared so freely. Did they know, he'd ask, how much bloody sweat he paid for those items or the electricity they switched on and off, like the wastrels they were? Despite their mother's warnings, Simon's brother would dash at their father each night as soon as he heard the key in the lock, with the greeting, "Hello Pa. Gimme a penny?" This was the cue for her father's most irritating refrain:

> You say you want a penny, *only* a penny. I've got dimes and quarters and half-dollars in my pockets, you say, so what's a penny to me? Well let's see. If you went to the El station and gave the man four cents, he wouldn't let you on the train, you'd need another penny. If Mama gave you two cents for a three-cent ice cream cone, would Mrs. Katz in the candy store give it to you? If Mama had only forty-eight cents for a forty-nine cent chicken, would the butcher give it to her?[1]

Even in childhood, Kate Simon had always recognized her father to be a frustrated, angry man who resented his children and considered them a burden. The anecdote of the penny confirmed the portrait of a man who had nothing to give. Simon was precociously aware of her father's limitations. More often, children and even adults deny their parents' failures until something concrete and objective like money forces recognition. Curiously, many of us are capable of rationalizing the most disturbing and disappointing aspects of our parents. Since we can't choose our parents and have little or no basis for comparison, we tend to accept anything they do as normal. The full force of recognizing that there's something wrong with their behavior seems to require a dramatic event, or the clarity of money. Even then, many people rationalize the revelations offered by money, so the shock of recognizing their failures or limitations is repeated again and again.

A fifty-five-year-old Baltimore attorney I'm acquainted with idealizes his long-dead parents. Nostalgically, Bob O'Connor recalls his father as the much respected "king" of the family, although he describes a man who was a tyrant: autocratic, controlling, and unwilling to allow any individuality in his three sons. "You must be like the three musketeers," the father would tell his sons as he groomed them to take over the hardware business he'd built up from nothing.

As a young man, O'Connor was unhappy and went into psychoanalysis, taking money from his father to pay the bills, a dependence that depressed him even further. Because of conflicts with his father, he had broken away from the family business and worked in corporate law. The father gradually relinquished control of his business to his sons as he grew older, giving each one an equal share. Because Bob was an "outside" owner, he didn't expect to draw the $75,000 salary (in the 1950s) his two brothers were paid from the business, but he did resent the fact that his brothers also helped themselves to fringe benefits: cars, restaurant meals, theater tickets, vacations—all charged to the business—which decreased the value of his shares.

When O'Connor expressed concern about the money that was being drawn from the company, one of his sisters-in-law retorted that her husband "sweat" to build the business while he did nothing for it. He found it useless to try to explain that salaries were different from the rights of shareholders. "Besides, you're a single person," his sister-in-law added, drawing now on different ammunition. "You don't need the money as much." "And then a very painful remark was made to me," he recalls. "My sister-in-law said, 'Isn't your father paying for your psychiatrist, and it's coming from the estate?' "

Eventually the business came into some extra cash when it sold a subsidiary, and the brothers offered to buy out O'Connor's shares. He agreed because he could see only a deteriorating situation in the future—more travel and restaurant expenses charged against the business and the looming threat of his brothers' sons who might eventually come in and demand shares of their own. But when the time came to arrange the transfer, he was shocked by what happened.

His brothers offered him $125,000, when even the conservatively stated book value indicated his shares were worth twice as much. So O'Connor turned to his father, who still had a dominating influence, and who had originally assured him that he was entitled to a third. "Strangely enough, my father reversed himself in front of me," he recalls with a shaking voice. "He said what I was being given was satisfactory. Now, why did he change? My father had built up his business and had great pride in it, and he was concerned about the business using so much of its money to buy me out that it might be in jeopardy. So now he judged things in terms of the strength of the business instead of what I deserved."

Ultimately O'Connor agreed to his brothers' terms because he decided it was worth sacrificing his fair share to stay on good terms with his family, the only family he has. Since then, he says, he's never had any money conflicts with them: "When we go out for dinner and they use the business card to pay for it, I throw in my money for my share of the bill, because I know money creates tensions." He also knows that he's had to pay his brothers to keep a place for himself in the family and this hurts him deeply. His story also illustrates how those who don't marry or have children are often treated as second-class citizens in their families and viewed as less deserving of money and support. However much parents talk about treating their children equally, those who don't "give back" to their parents by going into the family business or having children often discover, like this man at the restaurant, that they have to pay their own way.

Twenty-five years after the fact, Bob O'Connor is still visibly shaken at the realization that his father cared more about his business than he did about his son. To anyone less involved, it would have been obvious that a man who would ask his sons to be "the three musketeers" to preserve the integrity of his business is not leaving his business to his sons—he's leaving it to himself.

A midwestern woman I know, I'll call her Beth, was more willing to see the full implications of an incident involving her mother through its financial aspect. Beth grew up in a wealthy family, but after marrying and divorcing a man who fails to send child support payments, she finds herself, at age thirty-five, living on the edge—sometimes, even without phone service because she can't pay the bill. Recently, Beth's father, a prominent banker, died unexpectedly. A few days after the funeral, she visited her mother at her parents' summer home—a huge estate on Lake Michigan. At the train station, her mother greeted her with the announcement, "I'm giving your father's car to your brother because he needs a second car and you really can't afford to keep one in the city. I've made up my mind and I hope you won't try to argue with me." Several months later when Beth asked her mother for a $5,000 loan, her mother refused, saying she couldn't afford it because she'd just given Beth's brother $10,000 for the down payment on a house.

Beth had always regarded her father as her protector—but he'd left all his money to his wife, and now it was clear that Beth's mother had no intention of helping her either. Seeing the contrast between her mother's luxurious life-style and her own inability to buy her children badly needed winter coats, she can no longer maintain the fiction that her parents were ever genuinely concerned about her. At one time, she'd accounted for her terrible marriage on the grounds of naiveté—saying that when she married she was only twenty-one and assumed that all men were nice, like her father. Now she realizes she made a marriage that reproduced the rejection and withholding she'd always known since childhood. This woman was abandoned by both her father and her husband, and in each case she didn't realize it until the bills came due.

Another example of the revelatory power of money entails a man I know who comes from an old, puritanical New England family. He can barely recall spending any time with his stern, busy father, other than doing math exercises that his father considered educational or character-building. As a boy, John was a model child for his demanding father—brilliant in school, serious, thrifty, and a budding entrepreneur (he remembers that as a child he'd buy pencils in bulk, sharpen them and sell them for twice his cost at school). But despite his efforts he never received much affection from his father. When he turned twelve, he was given a checking account by his father, as an early lesson in financial planning, from which he had to buy all his clothes and school supplies. He always managed his account carefully, even saving a portion of it, though his allotment was meager compared to the allowances of his friends.

In 1960, when John was seventeen and about to leave home to go to Harvard, his father solemnly announced that he would give John $10,000 to cover four years worth of tuition, books, and living expenses, because he considered it his obligation to give his son a college education, but insisted that John had better manage the money wisely because he'd never get another penny from his father.

As it turned out, the warning was unnecessary. Already a compulsive saver, John worked throughout his years at Harvard, rarely spending a penny of his fund, and actually made it last through five more years as a graduate student. His most vivid memory of his father is the visit they paid to a stockbroker shortly before he left for college. His father had insisted on this outing to arrange for investing the money that was to pay for John's college years. After the stockbroker made his suggestions, and John had replied that he didn't really like them, his father impatiently drew the meeting to a close, snapping, "Well, do what he says anyway, and stop wasting the man's time." The memory hurts because it perfectly renders the father's attitude toward his son—he regarded the child as a wasteful demand on his own precious time.

Miraculously, John turned out to be an exceptionally sensitive and expressive man who is unusually involved and affectionate with his children. Though he's a successful professional, he jokes that he's still a tightwad, and he's never been able to shake off his anxiety about running out of money.

If money has the power to awaken some people to unpleasant realities, it also seems to be the case that other people, those who can't face finances at all, are often "deniers" in general—they make a habit out of avoiding the truth. Their discomfort with money, and the anxiety they suffer when they have to face it, is an indication of their fear about learning what they can't bear to know.

One can see it in the demeanor of some people when they sit down, once a month, to pay bills and write checks. They wear the expression of someone bracing for awful news. Then, having accomplished the task, their expression relaxes into deep relief, as if they've dodged a bullet. If it were merely the pain of spending money that made the task so dreadful, we should expect they'd look worse at the end of paying bills, but invariably the opposite is true. This is because their dread and inhibition springs not so much from facing the bills as from facing life itself—the look of peace at the end of the ordeal comes from having emerged alive, one more time, from a mortal confrontation.

An acquaintance of mine discovered after his father's death how reluctant the man was to deal with reality. His father had failed to leave a will because he'd been too weak to be truthful with his relatives. For years, the man had privately promised each of three people—his second wife and each of his two children from his first marriage—that he was leaving his house, his main asset, exclusively to them. Trapped by his lies, he couldn't write a will, so instead he left his heirs with conflicting promises and an estate that would have to be divided according to state law.

A successful commercial artist in the San Francisco Bay area whom I know provides another illustration of how denying reality is often behind a refusal to deal with money. The woman, now in her fifties, has earned several million dollars during the past twenty-five years and has managed to save most of it. She should have bought a house long ago—certainly she could have afforded to. But instead, she has lived all this time in a cramped, one-bedroom apartment still furnished with the bargains she found when she got her first apartment after college. She's unable to invite anyone for dinner because her table doubles as her desk and is always covered with papers, and her living room is filled with file cabinets. The apartment has only one closet, so the woman has to rotate her wardrobe by moving it back and forth from her elderly father's house; in winter she trades her cotton clothes for the woolens. Though she's great at making money she's hopeless at managing it, leaving that task to her father's accountant. That a woman of her accomplishments should live this way is remarkable, but she can't deal with money because it would force her to face some painful realities.

Mainly, she can't bear to face the fact that she has passed the age of fifty. Still tied to her father, she's never married, but is still looking for the right man. As she confessed in an unguarded moment, she's never bought a house because that would have been tantamount to accepting her condition as permanent—to seeing herself as an "old maid." She had never minded an apartment that looked like a temporary dwelling because she wanted to view it that way—as a place she was merely occupying until she got married. To buy a house was to settle into singlehood. As long as she lived like a girl just out of college, she could fool herself into thinking that time was not passing.

There are many people who find they can't save a penny though they earn a great deal because they, too, can't bear to face the reality of the future and the passing of time. To save money is indeed to provide for the future, but to do that, one must be able to imagine the future and project oneself into it. People who deny the circumstances of their lives must avoid any manner of taking stock. In his play *The Price*, Arthur Miller offers a fictional example of how a man's inability to earn money stemmed from a larger need to deny the truth about his family.

As the play opens, two middle-aged brothers meet for the first time after a long estrangement in order to sell the broken-down furniture that belonged to their parents, now dead. The older brother, a policeman, had been a loyal son—sacrificing a scientific education and career in order to work and support his father. The younger brother had gone his own way and become a rich and admired doctor, albeit a lonely one. In the course of the evening each one attacks the view of the family the other had carried through life, and its accompanying self-justifications—the policeman accusing his brother of selfishness, the doctor accusing his brother of masochism and self-deception.

As the story unfolds, we learn that the policeman had sacrificed his own life chances to retain a false image of the father, who was, in fact, a selfish and greedy man as the younger son always knew. In fact, the father had money stashed away all along. The career sacrifice made by the older son was entirely unnecessary—as he might have realized had he not been so blind to the faults of his father in his need to retain an image of a loving family. Charged with being selfish, the doctor accuses the policeman of using his sacrifice to justify his failure. Did the older brother fail to become a scientist, we're left to wonder, because he was a good son, or did he play the sacrificing son because he lacked the courage and confidence to compete in the world? The doctor, too, comes to see the price he's paid for living without illusions—he was free to break away from the family and succeed in the world, but his realism has left him a lonely man. The story implies that enduring relationships may require a few illusions.

The needs that blind us to a clear view of our parents obscure our vision just as much in the context of marriage. Here, too, money is the ingredient that often breaks the spell. In some cases, it's a romantic spell that's broken by the injection of realism that comes with specifying financial terms before marriage. A woman I know, a savings and loan banker, had been living with a man, also a bank executive, after each divorced their previous spouse. They'd been looking for a country house for weekends, but one day the man discovered and fell in love with a beautiful house on the ocean and insisted that they buy it. Although the house was a steal at the price, and owing to the desperation of the sellers they were able to get it for even less, it cost much more than they'd originally planned to spend. Cynthia Booth, the woman, was nervous about investing all her money in it. But she knew that her partner, having more money, would have more clout and could control how the house would be divided if they broke up. So, at the time they bought the house she insisted that they sign a legal contract that would specify the terms of dividing the property in case their relationship dissolved.

Cynthia's partner was furious at her insistence on the contract, hurt at her mistrust. "I'm fair and honorable," he complained, but she remembered how he'd talked about his wife and the division of their property when that marriage ended. Cynthia had lost most of her property in her first divorce and felt she needed the insurance of a contract in order to make another commitment.

In the end, they went to a matrimonial lawyer and signed a contract, but the negotiations were very bitter because of her partner's anger and Cynthia's mistrust. Actually, they almost broke up over the purchase of their dream house, and to this day, Cynthia fears that the contract permanently scarred their relationship because it shattered the romance for her partner.

It's my impression that when men are not the ones to propose a contract, they often take it badly if it's required of them, because they're less willing than women to acknowledge the unromantic aspects of marriage; being the ones who usually have the money and the power, they can afford to believe in romance. Despite the stereotype of women as the romantic sex, research has consistently shown that men's love for women often seems more tied to fantasies and illusions.[2] Women, being financially dependent, may have a greater need to be realistic. In the end, the reality testing forced by the contract bruised this relationship insofar as it was built on illusions. But eventually illusions are shattered, anyway.

Despite their romantic tendencies it's still usually men who want to have a prenuptial contract because it's typically the men who earn more money and want to reduce the share the state would award to their wives after a divorce. Women who outearn men are starting to insist on these contracts too. Yet most people find negotiating such an agreement an upsetting experience because it makes them confront the limits of their feelings for one another. According to a recent article about prenuptial agreements in Beverly Hills, it's awkward even when everyone's doing it:

> "If a guy with ten million dollars decides to marry a woman ten or fifteen years younger, she probably hasn't focused on the economics of her situation other than knowing it's going to be a nice life," says prominent Century City divorce lawyer to the stars Dennis Wasser. "Now that person sits down [at the prenuptial contract meeting] and realizes all the assets are going to stay separate property—that puts a new perspective on the person she's marrying. Conversely, the one with the money almost always thinks he's being married solely for his intellectual capacity, charm, or whatever, and then he realizes the other person is also interested in the economic aspects of the marriage, and that's very terrifying."[3]

As painful as it is to confront financial expectations, the alternative can be worse, as in the case of a woman I know who clung to her illusions until her selfish husband had wasted her entire inheritance. Jane Palmerino married a medical student when she was young and about the same time inherited $90,000 in 1965, when her mother died. Though her grandmother and aunts begged her to keep the money in her own name, she was undeterred in putting it in a joint account, because she believed people should bring trust and sharing into marriage. Over the years, her husband became increasingly abusive to her and a serious alcoholic. In ten years' time, her inheritance had been steadily reduced by his growing needs. First it was spent on yearly vacations in Europe to alleviate the tensions of being a medical student and resident. Then it was years of psychoanalysis because he was unhappy. As the money dwindled she was forced to confront the truth about the man. She'd been raised to believe that a man is supposed to protect his family, and this man was needing all the protection. It took her ten years to gather the conviction to ask for a divorce. By then, her original inheritance had dwindled from $95,000 to $30,000, and, to add insult to injury, her husband managed to take away half as part of the divorce settlement.

Wasting an inheritance is devastating. Those who do usually feel they've betrayed their parents and lost the final offering of parental care and protection. In a way, an inheritance can stand for what was best about a parent. It is pure care, pure love, pure provision of opportunity. At its best, an inheritance symbolizes one of the great gifts a parent can give—the opportunity for a child to do or become what she or he wants, and to choose without interference. Of course, much of the time, people are too afraid or too guilty to make use of the money to become something they really want, or they've never developed the personal qualities or discipline to succeed despite the financial provision. More often, they choose to use an inheritance as a final cloak of protection. The death of parents leaves many feeling naked in the world, shorn of a love and shelter they were able to believe in, whether or not it was truly there. To these people, it's unthinkable to spend the money that is bequeathed by a parent. Such money is for saving, for putting into very safe investments so they will always feel the warmth and security of parental care.

This is what Jane Palmerino, by temperament, would have done with her mother's money. As her husband continually dipped into the funds with assurances that once he was a doctor he could earn it all back, her protests that they shouldn't touch the capital were silenced. I asked her why she didn't stop him. "No woman in that era would have," she replied. And it was clear that she refused to see how she had volunteered herself for exploitation in this marriage.

Why did she do it? Probably because she couldn't bear to face the truth that her husband had married her not because he loved her but in order to use her. A needy person is willing to sacrifice anything, including an inheritance, to maintain the illusion of being loved. And yet, it was also the money that forced this woman to recognize the truth: while Jane Palmerino was still mourning her mother's death, it was her husband who insisted he was under stress and needed the money for therapy. She recalls:

> I said, "We don't have the money for it—that's seven thousand dollars a year." He said, "We have it." I said, "That's my inheritance." He said, "I need it, I'm unhappy." The money was symptomatic of his lack of strength, and the overall betrayal. He came to me for money and for his weakness. I had to ask, "How come my husband is weak and needs to take my money?" It showed that he couldn't take care of us, that he wasn't a man.

Her aunts and grandmother didn't make it any easier after her inheritance and her husband were gone. She begged them for a loan when she was desperate for money in the years following the divorce, but they were not forthcoming and only rubbed her nose in her shame. After all, they had warned her to keep the money in her own name. "And the saddest part," they would add, "is that your mother scrimped and saved pennies all her life so you would be independent and protected."

Now Palmerino talks a hard line about money, drilling her daughter with daily sermons about the importance of being financially independent. After the divorce, Palmerino returned to school, got an MBA, and now earns a good salary. She'd like to redeem her error by being able to leave her daughter a sizeable sum when she dies. And yet this new rhetoric sounds a bit hollow, because Palmerino is still unable to protect herself in relationships with men.

When I last saw her at a party, she cheerfully told the story of her current sacrifice. For years, she's been involved with a married man (although she's told me that what she really needs in a man is a social partner who's presentable in her professional circles).

After years of cautious discretion, her lover finally allowed her to come with him on a short business trip to Europe. Thrilled that their relationship had reached this new level of commitment, she eagerly awaited this trip and also looked forward to one wild day of shopping in Paris. But on the day she had planned to shop her lover got the flu, and being the self-sacrificer that she is, Palmerino spent the day holed up with him in their hotel room so that she could hold his head while he vomited.

I include this unsavory incident to illustrate the woman's masochism and her inability to face reality. The wasting of her mother's legacy was horribly painful for her, and yet her character has led her predictably to make endless accommodations for men who have little to give her. Although she's talented and resilient, she still clings to her illusions. On the one hand, the squandering of her inheritance forced her to acknowledge that she was being exploited by a husband who would never protect and provide for his family. But having gotten over one illusion, she now uses money to maintain another: the fiction that as long as a woman is financially independent, she protects herself from being exploited in love.

Money doesn't always bring rude awakenings. Often we're pleasantly surprised by the financial generosity of someone we love. The people I've described share a common, but not universal, vulnerability. For varying reasons, they were each deprived of parental love when young and those unfilled needs left them unprepared to protect or assert themselves in later loves. Those who were able to acknowledge the depth of their early disappointments were less shackled to illusions and more able to deal realistically with money and love.

3

——•——

Not Enough
to Go Around

One of the maxims of family life is that there's no need to compete, there's always enough to go around. Parents always say this to their children, many of whom would like to strangle each other, just as they say that they love all their children equally. But children are sensitive to the unadmitted preferences of their parents and there's no way to hide the differences in siblings' success in the world—in school, physical abilities, popularity.

People joke about sibling rivalry, but the seriousness of it is broadly denied. Even when siblings actually draw blood in a fight, the depth of feeling is dismissed as normal or at most touching, in that children unguardedly display the passions of jealousy adults learn to disguise. The rivalry is expressed not only in fights but in constant comparisons of who is getting more and who is getting less. "It's not fair" must be heard more than any other phrase in households containing children. The vigilance that children show over any sign of favoritism is not abandoned in later life, it's just not expressed so openly. For adults, money becomes the primary measure of love, and it is seen as love's reward.

The significance of sibling rivalry is causing many psychologists to revise their view of the family and its effect on people's personalities. Recent research[1] suggests that families don't provide identical climates for all siblings, and that the most important influence on the children's personalities may be their perception of how they compare with siblings. Parental preferences among children and the relative popularity of siblings among peers may

29

be the most formative experiences. Furthermore, research shows that children are acutely aware of parental discrimination between children that is so minor or subtle that the parents themselves don't notice it.

Despite parental assurances that there's enough to go around, children often learn that in the family love is scarce, or that sometimes one person is saved at the expense of another. Almost every woman I know who grew up with a sister recalls that one daughter was designated within the family as smart, and the other, pretty and feminine, and almost all have suffered lifelong problems because of these early distinctions. Perhaps their parents wanted to give each child the feeling of being special in some way, but each one registered, much more keenly, what she or he was not. In families, the market in any desirable trait is cornered very easily by just one person. To not be the prettiest daughter is the emotional equivalent of not being pretty at all. In families there are no gradations. Judgments are absolute. In this sense, the family is the most competitive place of all. In the outside world we recognize these judgments as matters of taste, or see that people are blessed with assets in degrees, along a continuum. In the family, the stakes are all or nothing, and there is no appealing to a different audience.

One of the biggest lies of family life is that children are loved equally. If it were so, and children believed it, why would they be so watchful for signs of preference, and remain so even into adulthood? Recently I spent an afternoon with a friend who assured me there were no favorites in her family. But we laughed when, riding in her car later that day, her eleven-year-old son kept nagging, "Mommy, tell me the truth, once and for all—who do you love most, me or Katy?" My friend insisted that she loved them equally but her son refused to believe this. Finally, to demonstrate her point, my friend asked her son, "Who do you love more, me or daddy?" and when he easily (and she knew, honestly) answered "Daddy," she flushed and retaliated. "Okay," joking but clearly a little hurt, "then I love Katy more."

The notion of loving one's children exactly the same is sacred in our culture, but logically unlikely. Individual children inevitably elicit different responses in their parents—some more loving than others. Whether on the basis of sex, physical resemblance, birth order, or temperament, parents often feel closer to, or more comfortable with, a particular child. Though this preference is usually denied, children always know whether or not they were favored—and carry the verdict with them all through life. Adrienne Rich, for example, has written about the mixed blessing of being a father's favorite daughter. In later life, Rich argues, she tends to be the "special" woman, perhaps the only woman in a world of men, but she also feels great pressure to please.[2] The daughter who is not favored probably never feels the confidence of her sister, but on the other hand, she's usually freer. Almost everyone I know has a clear sense of how they compared themselves with siblings in childhood, and believes those early distinctions had a deeply formative impact on their ways of getting along in life.

We carry these accidents of early childhood like maps into all future loves. As psychoanalysis suggests, we recognize or define love in terms of its resemblance to the original experience. As Freud so brilliantly demonstrated, most of us first experience love or disappointment in love in a context dominated by rival siblings and parents. Henceforth, love is always tied to rivalry. One of the most radical implications of Freud's insights is the fundamentally competitive nature of the family. Why do grown children fight over their dead parents' old furniture, asks the antiques dealer in Miller's play *The Price*. "Because," he explains, "even from high-class people you wouldn't believe the shenanigans—five hundred dollars they'll pay a lawyer to fight over a bookcase worth fifty cents—because you see, everybody wants to be number one."[3]

A woman I know was well aware throughout childhood of how much she disliked her younger sister, and of resenting her sister's relationship with their parents. Ann Daniel's parents are terribly controlling—and both of their daughters, now in their forties, are still struggling to gain their independence. Both women are artists, and find it hard to live comfortably on their small earnings. Their father keeps each on the dole—never giving them enough to be independent, but always enough to keep them coming back for more. Ann has noticed that taking money from her parents always entails the obligation of having more contact with them than she wants. The money is always tied to obligatory visits, phone calls, or agreeing with their opinions.

For years, Ann tried to resist her dependence on her parents and at times refused an offer of money, knowing it carried the obligation of contact. But when she observed that her sister, who phones their mother every day to gossip about the relatives, mysteriously came up with the down payment for a condominium, she felt cheated. When she turned forty, Ann adopted a little boy and secured her place as the favorite daughter. She smiles at the thought that she is the one who provided a grandchild for her parents, and especially that she's the one who gave her father the son he always wanted. "It's what's keeping him alive," she tells me. Now, after twenty years of struggling to be free of her parents, she has a good reason to depend on them for child care, advice, money. She rationalizes the weekly trips to her parents' house on the grounds that her son needs a father figure, and her father is the only one who's currently available. By giving her father a son she has finally won the competition with her sister, and with it, the spoils.

In the Freudian view of the family, the most intense rivalries are waged not between siblings, but between parent and child. Feminists often point to the ways that women are undermined by their fathers (and other powerful men) when these men don't take them seriously. Perhaps we've overlooked how sons are even more savagely undermined by their fathers precisely because the sons are viewed as the serious contenders. And remarkably, fathers can be fully unaware of the absurdly competitive attitude they show toward their sons. I know a highly successful and driven lawyer who, for years, forced his son (who was indifferent to sports) to play tennis with him so he could flex his muscles on the court. Now, he cloaks his rivalry by constantly expressing concern over his son's future. In fact, his son is an outstanding student at Stanford Law School and shows every sign that he will be a great success. But his father repeatedly worries that his son probably won't do as well as he has, and surely this will ruin the boy's life. The more the son distinguishes himself, the more the father worries about his son's future, for unconsciously he's really worried that his son will outperform him.

An equally driven professional investor I know similarly confided his hope that his sons won't follow in his footsteps "because the standard would be so high, they'd fail. This is a profession" he adds. "We're not dealing with a family business or product being sold to the public, where if you're a little weaker than your father it doesn't matter." Between fathers and sons, the competition is mixed up with mutual identification, and the blend of the two is often expressed through financial success—money. If daughters unconsciously model their love experiences on what happened to their mothers, sons seem to inherit their fathers' competitiveness and fear of failing.

An example that comes to mind is a man I know who was the oldest son in an upper-class WASP family. As a child, Philip Sims was constantly sermonized by his father about the importance of hard work and achievement. Although Philip did extremely well in school, his father was never satisfied. "Your reach should always exceed your grasp," was Mr. Sims's motto. Eventually Philip went into the publishing business, which was respectable work for someone of his background, but not terribly lucrative. On his thirty-fifth birthday his father took him to lunch and initiated a serious talk, telling him that he had about five more years to make it, because in business, if you weren't on the fast track by the time you were forty, you weren't going to be a success.

As Philip recalled, the discussion left him with a "sickening feeling that I was going to be a failure because I had no plans to make it by forty." Years later, he realized his father had said these things because he hadn't "made" it himself. As in many families of this class, the wealth and social standing of the family really derived from the success of an ancestor rather than the achievements of the current generation. Philip's father had done reasonably well—he'd preserved the money he inherited from his own father and made a good salary as an advertising executive—but at forty Philip's father saw that he was being passed over for positions at the top of his corporation and so resigned from the company to preserve his dignity.

Like many men who inherit money, Philip's father was plagued with worries about being a failure and made his son feel like a failure, too. Philip recalls that once while watching a performance of the ballet *The Prodigal Son*, he'd nearly burst into tears at the sight of the wastrel son, ragged and humiliated, dragging himself home after defying his father and prematurely spending his inheritance. In the ballet, as the broken son crawls across the stage to his exalted father, the old man opens his arms in forgiveness. Philip believes he was crying at the image of a forgiving father, but obviously he was affected, too, by the shame of the son who had failed to live up to his father's expectations. Not long after his father warned him that he had only a few years left to make something of himself, Philip quit the publishing business and joined an advertising firm much like the one his father had resigned from. Though he is more aware than his father of the self-doubts they hold in common, he is equally driven by a compulsion to demonstrate his worth, measured in dollars and cents.

Family businesses and their characteristic problems offer another window into the significance of money in the rivalry between fathers and sons. It's a well-known problem of family businesses that fathers have a hard time transferring control to their sons, especially when they were the original entrepreneurs. Frequently, the entrepreneur surrounds himself with weak people and can't bear to let his son take over while he's still alive. As an old man, he wants to "die in the saddle," while his middle-aged son guiltily waits in the wings for the death that will free him to become a man.

Consciously or unconsciously these fathers often make sure their sons will never outperform them. It's a common practice, for example, for fathers to bury their sons in the shipping department, or withhold vital information from them. Partly the problem is their absolute need to control everything in the business that has become the extension of their selves. But there's also the equation that if their sons take over, they must step down. In their minds, there's room for only one man at the top.

In one case I know, a father tried not to repeat with his own son the relation he'd had with his father. He's sure he has succeeded, though he deceives himself badly. My acquaintance, Kevin Gallagher, recalls his father as a tyrant both in the family and at work—actually there was no distinction between the two realms, because the senior Gallagher employed all his own brothers and sisters (Kevin's uncles and aunts) in his business, and to all he dished out a great deal of abuse. Toward his son, he displayed an absurd rivalry. Kevin recalls that on the rare nights his father came home for dinner if he noticed that his wife had cooked peas for his son because the boy didn't like spinach, he would complain, "You're making him something different?"

As a youth, Kevin craved contact with his much-absent father (who was discovered upon his death to have been leading a double life with a mistress). At age nineteen he was finally permitted to work in one of the smaller firms his father owned, but the operations of the business always seemed irrational and mysterious because his father failed to tell him that certain agreements had been made with mobsters.

After a year, Kevin left his father's business out of frustration, married, and became partners with his father-in-law, using money he secretly borrowed from his mother to buy out the previous partner. Now he transferred all the suppressed hatred and rivalry he'd felt for his father to his father-in-law, and by working like a maniac, within a few years managed to tyrannize and squeeze the kind old man out of his beloved business. He has built up the business dramatically, and Kevin's brothers-in-law are, today, his employees—working for salaries in the furniture manufacturing company their father founded. Like his father before him, Kevin controls everyone in the family. Furthermore, after taking over her father's business, he divorced his wife, so his brothers-in-law are now working for an employer who is no longer a member of their family. About the divorce, Kevin offers an ironic explanation:

After the kids were out of the house we had no problems, and family life is solidified by problems. In the old days we each had a grandmother in a nursing home, and we had aunts, uncles, grandparents dying of cancer, hospitalizations. All of a sudden the people are dead, the children are gone, you're affluent, and the solidarity you once had over problems isn't there and you find you have nothing in common.

But once he was divorced, a strange thing happened to this driven man. With his father-in-law dead and his wife out of the picture, he totally lost interest in the business—the obsession that had dominated his life. Having never been on his own, he was also in a panic and a deep depression. For two years, he let the business slide, and then he started to force his own son to come in and save it.

Kevin's son, Mark, had just earned a degree in architecture and gotten a job he loved in a Los Angeles architectural firm. He had also just married a fashion designer, a marriage his father envied. "I wish I could find a girl like that," Kevin, at fifty, would say, when he tried to persuade his twenty-five-year-old son to include him in the couple's social life and fix him up with one of their

young friends. Mark begged for two more years at his job so he
could be certified as an architect, but Kevin threatened that if he
didn't come into the business immediately there would be no business for him to inherit. Finally, Mark yielded, and Kevin made
him a full partner to demonstrate how different he was from his
own father. Mark has a different view of the event: "My father was
jealous that I was working long hours for an architect I really
admired."

As Kevin sees it, he gave his son the greatest gift a father can
give—what he himself had always wanted and never gotten from
his own father, an equal partnership in the business. As for forcing his son out of his chosen profession he can't see the sacrifice,
and minimizes it: "Architecture and furniture aren't that different. When you're an architect, you're in a business, like mine.
You're not doing that much design—you're dealing with customers and doing business. You're only creating about five percent of
the time. And I was letting him do our designing, whatever he
wanted. It wasn't like I was starting him in the shipping department."

By forcing his son into the business, Kevin Gallagher not only
lured Mark away from architecture and a rival father-figure, he
also lured his son away from his mother. Until he was forced into
his father's business, Mark had been closer to his mother after his
parents' divorce. Now that he had to see his father every day at
work, he naturally saw less of his mother.

At the beginning of their partnership the father and son fought
over everything, including how many hours make up a work day.
If Mark wasn't the first one in and the last one out of the factory,
Kevin felt abandoned. By the end of the first year, Mark was
putting in long days while Kevin rarely came to the factory. Instead, Kevin now devotes himself to decorating his new loft—a
nearly exact replica of his son's. And Kevin's new girlfriend is
even younger than his daughter-in-law.

Generous with his money, Kevin fails to see his deeper greed.
Not only did he use money to draw Mark away from his mother
and his profession, but after forcing Mark to assume his place in
the business, Kevin has taken over his son's former life. "He'd be
glad if I took over completely," Mark observes, "because he'd like
to be me." In effect, Kevin has turned his son into his father, so he
can enjoy the youth he never had.

If fathers and sons often use money as weapons in their rivalry, mothers and daughters, usually lacking money, have traditionally used love. Some time ago, I had the opportunity to observe an interesting contest between a mother and daughter that was ostensibly over money, but as in the case of so many personal competitions, had love at its core.

Julie Pastella had inherited a small jewelry business in Boston from her father, Joe Fallon, when he died of cancer. The business was worthless from a financial viewpoint, but it held great sentimental value for Julie, an only child who had been her father's main joy in life. Her mother had always been the outsider in the family. She was an unpleasant woman, unloving and unloved. Growing up, Julie had always worked with her father in the little store after school and on weekends. The two had made it their real home, away from her mother. Even after Julie got married, had children, and divorced, she'd returned to work for her father at the store and her father, she knew, had stayed in his unhappy marriage so he could afford to help support his daughter and grandchildren.

A couple of years before he died, Mr. Fallon had informally separated from his wife, whose behavior had grown progressively more disturbed, and moved into his own apartment. As he lay dying in the intensive care unit, his estranged wife showed up and served him with divorce papers. Recognizing how disturbed she was, Mr. Fallon then changed his will just days before he died, giving his daughter total ownership of the jewelry store (rather than the original 75 percent), so that she wouldn't be saddled with her mother as a business partner. After he died, Julie's mother challenged the new will and took her daughter to court, claiming that Julie had manipulated her father into changing the will when he was no longer of sound mind.

To prove that she and her husband still had a close marriage, and thereby build her case of manipulation, Mrs. Fallon produced a greeting card sent by her husband from the hospital, on which he'd written, "Dear Rose, I hope you find the happiness you've always looked for. Love, Joe." Julie had a greeting card that she'd received from her mother that she might have used to demonstrate her mother's insanity, but she kept it to herself. On the first Father's Day after Joe Fallon's death, her mother had sent her a photograph of her father working in the store, and had scrawled all across it in red ink, "Happy Father's Day."

Even without that bit of evidence, the judge quickly perceived the situation, and dismissed the jury and the case against Julie, allowing the final will to stand. A week later, something extremely disturbing happened to Julie. The jewelry store was robbed at gunpoint, and before the holdup men left, they sprayed the walls and display counters with 45-caliber bullets. The circumstances pointed to a theft arranged by someone who knew the business well. Instead of asking for the new and more valuable gold jewelry in the display cases (which Julie could have easily replaced with the insurance), the holdup men had emptied out the safe where customers' watches and rings were stored while being cleaned or repaired. As a result, Julie now had to face a few hundred customers who were terribly upset at learning they would never again see a possession that held sentimental value. Not only did Julie risk losing regular customers, but she feared for her safety since some of her customers had criminal backgrounds and a few had shouted violently when told their jewelry was gone. Julie's boyfriend, who worked with her in the store, decided he wanted nothing more to do with it and told her she could choose between keeping the store and keeping him. Although she'd never know for sure, she couldn't rule out the possibility that her mother might have arranged the holdup. It sickened her to think her own mother might have done this.

Mrs. Fallon had ostensibly gone to court to sue for shares of a profitless business, but her real fury stemmed from being displaced by her daughter in her husband's heart. And when she held up her greeting card to claim that love, she was thrown out of court.

We like to think of the family as a peaceful harbor, a shelter in the storm. Everything in us resists the idea that this sacred little circle could be disturbed by conflicts of interests, competition, and rage. But cruelty is a part of human nature as well as love, and the family, with its intense attachments, dependencies, and power imbalances, is a breeding ground for all kinds of private cruelties—and one that is hard to leave.

Fortunately, most families are at least a mixed bag. Even Julie had her affectionate father to counteract the disturbed rage of her mother. And Kevin and Mark Gallagher have a surprisingly workable relationship in their business, because after years of family therapy Mark has learned to understand his father's competitiveness, and Kevin has learned to channel his competitiveness into a more helpful and constructive partnership with his son. Still, as Arthur Miller's furniture dealer concluded, the insoluble problem is that everyone wants to be number one. It's hard to admit this among people you're supposed to love, so we fight over money instead.

4

———•———

The Cash Nexus

*P*eople like to say that money corrupts. Behind this sentiment is the conviction that we prostitute ourselves when we sell those things that should be above any price. The spoiling, degrading aspect of money stems from this. Money has the power to rob things of their personal, emotional, or aesthetic values because these qualities and whatever else is uniquely valuable about something cannot be measured in dollars.

The tension between monetary value or price and other values, between the economic and noneconomic aspects of life, was a central concern of nineteenth-century European philosophers like Georg Simmel and Karl Marx who observed how the diffusion of the market mentality had transformed all human ties in modern life. Like Marx, Simmel feared that this dehumanizing "cash nexus" would infiltrate all human relations.

In his 1900 treatise, *The Philosophy of Money*,[1] Simmel argued that although we value what is personally unique and distinctive, the market tends to invade even the most sacred areas of life, trivializing and destroying them. He was especially intrigued by the kind of degradation that he saw in prostitution or its more respectable counterpart, marriage for money. Marriage for money, he observed, is like prostitution, because what is most personal and distinct is traded for a price.

In contemporary middle-class American life, a similar cheapening of what is personal and emotional is experienced by many people in psychotherapy when they hand a check to their therapist: there is a disturbing disjuncture between pouring one's heart out to another and having to pay for this by the hour. An older

41

generation of psychoanalysts used to try to separate money payments from the therapeutic session by sending a monthly bill in
the mail. But today, many younger therapists ask for their payment at the end of each appointment so they don't have to deal
with the problems of collecting their fees.

According to Simmel, putting a price on anything personal is
somewhat corrupting because at the moment that something distinct is given a monetary value its qualitative worth becomes subordinated to its quantitative value—an extraneous standard has
been forced upon it. To understand how price supersedes qualitative value, consider the value of a house.

A house used to be regarded as a highly personal object—the
setting for one's entire life. Not so long ago, when people bought
a house they expected to live there forever. People didn't begin
with "starter" homes to get into the market. Today, people don't
buy a home, they buy a piece of real estate, basing their choices on
what's likely to go for the best price in the future. If they consider
adding a bathroom or a porch, they calculate how much the improvement will add to the resale value. As in other intimate connections, the once personal relationship a person had with his or
her house has been degraded into a more calculating, exploitative, short-term association. There's a tie between monetizing
objects and viewing them as short-term investments. On this
theme, Simmel observed that money depersonalizes relationships
because paying for something has the effect of freeing the buyer
from a more enduring attachment or engagement with the seller.
We have all observed how giving a personally chosen present has
a more intimate quality than giving a cash gift: it signifies a more
personal bond between giver and receiver. This is one reason why
Simmel regarded the transaction involved in prostitution as a metaphor for all modern relationships. As in prostitution, having
paid for a service, one is free to leave—there is no further obligation on the part of the buyer. Anthropological studies support
Simmel's observation. There is cross-cultural evidence that when
people pay immediately for a service, the relationship tends to be
a short-term one. Accounts can be left uneven when people expect the relationship to continue.

In short, the basic thrust of money is to free the individual, for
better or worse, from being dependent on or responsible for relationships with specific other people. With money, I may buy

what I wish from any number of people. My life and my choices are no longer controlled by parents, spouse, community. Having money I may choose and move on to other people, other places. My money carries value in any market, and if I can't buy what I want from one person, I can buy it from another.

So money is a double-edged sword. It is alienating, and it trivializes what is most personal and unique, but it also liberates the individual who would otherwise be embedded in a web of inescapable relationships. In relationships, money provides freedom. As in prostitution, not only does the payment complete the relationship, but it gives the buyer a choice. Since the same service can be bought from any number of people, in modern life money enlarges the circles of people who can provide what we want or need. In his novel *Howard's End* E. M. Forster's heroine makes this very observation: "The poor cannot always reach those whom they want to love, and they can hardly ever escape from those they love no longer. We rich can."[2]

In this way, money is the basis of personal autonomy. Mistakenly, we tend to think of autonomy as a trait or capacity that's deeply rooted in the personality, perhaps a product of early socialization. But traits like autonomy or dependence are not merely or necessarily fixed in one's character—they are also reflections of our position or status.

Virginia Woolf brilliantly posed this point in her essay *A Room of One's Own*. Writing in 1929, Woolf asked why there have been no female Shakespeares, and concluded that for creative genius to reach its fullest development, a woman, like a man, must have a fixed and independent income, and the material surroundings that nurture genius.

To illustrate how differently men and women are nurtured, Woolf conjured up two visits and two meals she'd taken, one at "Oxbridge"—the university for privileged young men—and one at the modest college attended by their sisters. Visiting the men's school, she wandered through golden meadows, along peaceful rivers, past magnificent buildings that had served for centuries as sanctuaries for great thinkers and ambitious works. Yet when she tried to enter the Oxbridge library, her passage was barred before she could step through the door. At the Oxbridge library, women were not allowed. As she surveyed the foundation of gold and silver on which this great male university was built, the clock struck and it was time to join the male faculty for their customary meal, all of which allowed her to reflect on how luxury affects one's attitude:

> The lunch on this occasion began with soles, sunk in a deep dish, over which the college cook had spread a counterpane of the whitest cream, save that it was branded here and there with brown spots like the spots on the flanks of a doe. After that came the partridges . . . many and various . . . with all their retinue of sauces and salads, the sharp and the sweet, each in its order; their potatoes, thin as coins but not so hard; their sprouts, foliated as rosebuds but more succulent. And no sooner had the roast and its retinue been done with than the silent serving-man . . . set before us, wreathed in napkins, a confection which rose all sugar from the waves. To call it pudding and so relate it to rice and tapioca would be an insult. Meanwhile the wine-glasses had flushed yellow and flushed crimson; had been emptied; had been filled. And thus by degrees was lit, half-way down the spine, which is the seat of the soul, not that hard little electric light which we call brilliance . . . but the more profound, subtle and subterranean glow, which is the rich yellow flame of rational intercourse. No need to hurry. No need to sparkle. No need to be anybody but oneself. We are all going to heaven and Vandyck is of the company—in other words, how good life seemed, how sweet its rewards, how trivial this grudge or that grievance, how admirable friendship and the society of one's kind, as, lighting a good cigarette, one sunk among the cushions in the window-seat.[3]

If such a meal produces warmth and expansiveness, how does one feel, she wondered, when living on a tight budget? That night she dined at the women's college, an institution built not on foundations of gold and silver (for women have had little money with which to endow their institutions), but on the meager sums that could be scraped up each year:

> Here was the soup. It was a plain gravy soup. There was nothing to stir the fancy in that. One could have seen

through the transparent liquid any pattern that there might have been on the plate itself. But there was no pattern. The plate was plain. Next came beef with its attendant greens and potatoes—a homely trinity, suggesting the rumps of cattle in a muddy market, and sprouts curled and yellowed at the edge. . . . Prunes and custard followed. . . . Biscuits and cheese came next, and here the waterjug was liberally passed round, for it is the nature of biscuits to be dry, and these were biscuits to the core. That was all. The meal was over. Everybody scraped their chairs back; the swingdoors swung violently to and fro; soon the hall was emptied of every sign of food and made ready no doubt for breakfast next morning . . . Conversation for a moment flagged. The human frame being what it is, heart, body and brain all mixed together, and not contained in separate compartments as they will be no doubt in another million years, a good dinner is of great importance to good talk. One cannot think well, love well, sleep well, if one has not dined well. The lamp in the spine does not light on beef and prunes. We are all *probably* going to heaven, and Vandyck is, we *hope*, to meet us round the next corner—that is the dubious and qualifying state of mind that beef and prunes at the end of the day's work breed between them.[4]

And so, Virginia Woolf went to bed, pondering what effects wealth and poverty have on the mind, thinking of "the safety and prosperity of the one sex and of the poverty and the insecurity of the other and of the effect of tradition and the lack of tradition upon the mind of the writer."[5]

Later in her essay, Woolf describes how she was changed by an inheritance. In 1918, her aunt died, leaving her an income of 500 pounds a year for the rest of her life. The news of the inheritance reached her about the same time as the news that women had finally won the right to vote. Of the two events, she had no doubt that the money would be the more important one in her life. Before the inheritance she'd been forced to do work she hated, "flattering and fawning," like a slave, while her true gift for writing was perishing, and with it her soul:

All this became like a rust eating away the bloom of the spring, destroying the tree at its heart. However, as I say,

my aunt died; and whenever I change a ten-shilling note
a little of that rust and corrosion is rubbed off; fear and
bitterness go. Indeed, I thought, slipping the silver into
my purse, it is remarkable, remembering the bitterness of
those days, what a change of temper a fixed income will
bring about. No force in the world can take from me my
five hundred pounds. Food, house and clothing are mine
forever. Therefore not merely do effort and labour cease,
but also hatred and bitterness. I need not hate any man;
he cannot hurt me. I need not flatter any man; he has
nothing to give me. So imperceptively I found myself
adopting a new attitude towards the other half of the human race. It was absurd to blame any class or any sex, as
a whole.[6]

Other novelists, searching for a love that is pure of economic
motives, have explored how money corrupts. But Woolf's essay
reminds us that the absence of money can corrupt even more.

Anyone who doubts the role that money plays in the relations
between the sexes need only consider the large proportion of
American husbands and wives who stay in unhappy marriages
because they can't afford to leave them. Every study of the impact
of income on divorce rates has shown a clear relationship between
financial dependence and loyalty: as women earn more money,
they're more likely to ask for a divorce. In fact, we take for granted
the assumption that persons with money have certain "rights"
over their dependents. "I'm paying for it, so I have the right to
choose," a parent will say to a child after every other explanation
has been exhausted. It may be voiced less openly between adults,
but it's understood by most couples that the one who contributes
more money also has the right to choose. In American family life,
the one who pays feels entitled to all sorts of rights, not only in
decisions about what to buy and how to live but also rights to sex
and attention. We take these rights so much for granted that we
barely question them, though we insist that the family is nothing
like the marketplace.

The idea that money really stands behind qualities (be they
autonomy, authority, beauty, freedom, or genius) that we take to
have an independent existence was articulated most forcefully by
Karl Marx. In a poetic short essay on "The Power of Money" Marx

explained how the ability of the rich to buy anything gives them unlimited power in all realms.

> My power is as great as the power of money. The proper-
> ties of money are my own (the possessor's) properties and
> faculties. What I *am* and *can do* is, therefore, not at all my
> individuality. I *am* ugly, but I can buy the most beauti-
> ful woman for myself. Consequently I am not *ugly*, for
> the effect of ugliness, its power to repel, is nullified by
> money. . . . I am a detestable, dishonourable, unscrupulous
> and stupid man, but money is honoured, and so also is its
> possessor. Money is the highest good and so its possessor is
> good.[7]

Not only can money purchase all capacities a person could want, observed Marx, but it even has the power to make things seem their opposite, thereby rendering genuine distinctions almost meaningless. On this point he quoted Shakespeare, who spoke of how gold can "make black white, foul fair, wrong right, base no-ble, old young." Oddly enough, in our own times, we recognize this transformative power in only one thing other than money: love. If money can turn foul into fair, so can love, according to our myths, turn the beast into a prince.

More recently, Pierre Bourdieu, a French sociologist, has ex-amined how money and class even stand behind what we regard as personal taste. Looking at contemporary French style and cul-ture, he observes how a person's choice of clothing, food, body type, furniture, leisure activities, and other matters of "taste" are distinctions that are always made in opposition to the choices made by members of other classes. Taste does not flow from truly per-sonal inclinations but rather expresses our sense of place in the class of structure. Every time we express a "personal" preference, we actually express class membership.

Taste, Bourdieu argues, falls along the lines of two major ori-entations. In all matters, the rich wish to display a taste of luxury and freedom, while the poor are forced to settle for a taste of necessity. While the poor are ever concerned with function (whether a coat will be practical, a meal filling, shoes durable), the rich display a taste that scorns function for form, that distin-guishes itself from the taste of the poor by being refined by style and as distant from necessity as possible. The two class-based orientations to function versus form appear in preferences in art, furniture, manners, and food:

> In opposition to the free-and-easy working class meal, the bourgeoisie is concerned to eat with all due form. Form is first of all a matter of rhythm, which implies expectations, pauses, restraints: waiting until the last person served has started to eat, taking modest helpings, not appearing over-eager. A strict sequence is observed. . . . Before the dessert is served, everything left on the table, even the salt-cellar, is removed, and the crumbs are swept up.[8]

In other words, when food and dress are valued for their form and style rather than their function, they become sensual objects, not mere necessities.

Of course, the relationship between class and taste involves more distinctions and subtleties. In some matters, American upper-class WASPS will eschew a taste for luxury to further distinguish themselves from the middle class and newly rich. Thus many American WASP men with inherited wealth prefer to order "practical" leisure clothes from the L. L. Bean catalogue. They're not worried about being confused with the poor in choosing practical clothes. It's from the vulgar rich they need to be distinguished. For the same reason, some people with old money wouldn't be caught dead in a Mercedes or a BMW. Of course, in other aspects of their manners and bearing they studiously avoid ever displaying an attitude of "necessity"—practicality is one thing, but necessity is another. Similarly, some who are poor will display a taste for luxury rather than necessity in their choice of automobile, for example, a Cadillac. They, too, are trying to distance themselves from the class (the really poor) they're most likely to be confused with.

The financial basis of taste extends even into love. As Bourdieu documents, "Taste is a match-maker; it marries colours and also people, who make 'well-matched couples'."[9] The social critic Theodor Adorno also observed that sexual attraction is a function of money. Forty years ago he wrote, "The quality of every one of the countless automobiles which return to New York on Sunday evenings corresponds exactly to the attractiveness of the girl sitting in it."[10] Today, people joke about the "marriage market" and acknowledge there is buying and selling. Yet how fully do we recognize how much we measure ourselves and each other in terms of market value?

In the days of dowries, bride prices, and arranged marriages, the economic basis of marriage was explicit. But the contemporary middle class, with its ideology of romance, would like to believe that marriage is made on the basis of attraction to personal traits and values. In fact, however, most people choose partners from identical social backgrounds—despite the belief that people fall in love because of personal characteristics. The economic basis of love and marriage is revealed not only by the fact that people almost always marry within their class, but that when they marry out of it, it's because they've obviously traded one asset—youth, beauty, fame—for another: how often does one see a *poor*, older man with a rich, young lover, male or female?

Even the young, who have the undeserved reputation for rebelling against social conventions when it comes to love, typically choose partners on the basis of rational calculation. In surveys and experiments, social psychologists have found[11] that college students choose dates according to certain "equity" principles. They perceive their own market value in terms of their assets—background, money, looks, achievement, talents—and choose a partner with a matching value. The studies show, furthermore, that there's remarkable consistency among judges in rating a person's market value.

The basis of a "'good" match varies by class. The American middle class, being obsessed with social and economic mobility, evaluates a good marriage in exactly these terms. A desirable partner is one who can provide money or contacts with a higher class. The tie between love and social mobility has been one of the great themes of novels depicting the psychological orientation of the middle-class hero. Novelists like Balzac, Stendhal, Flaubert, and F. Scott Fitzgerald often took as their theme the "sentimental education" of a male hero whose illusions about love invariably meshed with his social ambitions and admiration for the upper class. For these fictional heroes, falling in love with a rich woman was indistinguishable from their admiration for the class they aspired to. Their loss of illusions about love coincided with their education about the power of money. In the end, they discovered that money had created the illusion of beauty, grace, intelligence, style, and dignity, which they had naively perceived as the special qualities of the rich.

It has been frequently observed that the first Jewish, male faculty members at Harvard University who were allowed to achieve senior positions were often married to the daughters of the upper-class WASP establishment they were pushing against. Extremely ambitious and competitive, these intellectuals from poor backgrounds invariably picked wives who were blonde, thin, well-groomed, and well-connected—the kinds of women who could help them gain acceptance in an elite world traditionally closed to Jews.

"It was a tradition among the New York intellectuals to marry money," says Irving Kristol, explaining how a generation of liberal male writers in the 1940s and 1950s were able to afford a life in New York.[12] In the 1960s it was common for radical leaders to become involved with women who had big trust funds. One man I know who was a major figure in the civil rights and antiwar movements made the rounds of movement women who came from rich, powerful families. Today, he's married to the daughter of a manufacturer whose politics he abhors. Yet he loves his father-in-law and is on such close terms with him that his wife complains that she's completely ignored when they visit. Like many fictional heroes who are upwardly mobile, his attraction to the daughter was largely motivated by his ambivalent attraction to the father and his need to compete with him. Today, one of the great disappointments of heterosexual, black female college students is that they have no one to date. Many of the black male students are more interested in having white girlfriends as symbols of their success, and the black women are overlooked by white males as well.

Whatever their other identifications, men have traditionally been able to trade their talent and promise for access to a "better" family—achieving a position in the class they often claim to have contempt for. This is true not only for rebels and intellectuals but men who simply want to get ahead. One divorce lawyer I know got married when he was a promising law student because his wife's family could help him with his career. It might just as well have been an arranged marriage. His mother gave him money for the diamond engagement ring, and her mother came along with the couple to help them pick it out. Forty-five judges came to his wedding, all invited by his father-in-law (a judge himself) and when he started to practice law, most of his business came from referrals from his wife's family.

Money is also a strong component of love for the rich. The reason members of the upper classes marry money has less to do with ambition or mobility than with preserving a way of life and distinguishing themselves as members of a restricted society. While for the middle class, marrying money is tied to the overriding concern with individual achievement, for the upper class, marrying money is aimed at retaining and restoring an image, not creating one. As Simmel observed, the middle class is forever expanding and is open at both ends, while the upper class remains closed and exclusive. While middle-class people identify themselves and each other according to individual achievement, in the upper class, identity is based on membership and background— family lineage, schools, travel, clubs. Except for the few who manage to truly distinguish themselves by some personal achievement, members of the upper class *are* their schools, clubs, families. As Simmel observed, the common conditions of their privileged lives, (summer houses, elite schools, travel, restricted clubs) extend so deeply into their identities that they are brought into relationships as self-evident assumptions. That is why Simmel argued that aristocrats "often get to know one another better in an evening than the middle class would in a month."

An acquaintance of mine who makes much of his family background describes what a well-matched pair he made with his first wife, though now they are divorced:

> My wife was from an identical class. Our grandfathers were in the same undergraduate class at Yale. Both of our fathers went to Yale; our mothers went to the same prep school. Our financial situations were even. Both of us have summer houses in the family. Both families have old furniture. Both of our fathers were executives in large corporations and both mothers were in the Junior League and did volunteer work. We were a perfect match for one another, except emotionally.

Not discouraged by his first mistake, this man assumes that when he remarries, he will pick another woman from his class.

Who else, he asks, would understand the intricacies of living off a trust fund?

For families with money that has passed through several generations, the fear of losing it plays a major role in marriage and child rearing. Since identity is so tied to the money and the memberships it provides, and since the money has not been personally earned and is therefore not so easily replaced, there is customarily an absolute prohibition on "spending down capital"—a rule taught early and severely enforced. Usually it is understood that where money has passed through generations, each one may use the interest but the principal should be left intact for future generations. In this sense, the inheritance belongs to the family as a whole and to generations yet unborn. Children learn that to break this rule is to disobey one of the deepest moral principles of the family, for it is only by guarding the inviolability of that capital that the family can retain its position. Only their capital protects them from the indignities of life among the masses. The thought of living without money is so terrifying, the shame of losing it so great, that almost every person I interviewed who came from a long-rich family mentioned at least one relative who had committed suicide after losing family funds. One woman I know, who lost her inheritance in a divorce settlement, recalled being so humiliated at having to beg for a loan from Harvard Law School when she was a student there that she blurted out, "You don't understand—I'm one of you."

There are tax angles, also, in preserving capital. Inheritance taxes may be reduced if a fortune is left in trust for grandchildren, or if trusts are arranged giving children only the interest on the principal. Such an arrangement keeps inheritance taxes down, since they are paid only once in three generations. Naturally, this tax dodge creates an odd relationship between generations. It's often joked that upper-class grandparents get revenge on their children by skipping a generation in their wills and leaving their money in trust for the grandchildren, to be distributed when their children die. Although tax considerations are probably the major motive for arranging trusts this way, the unintended consequences illustrate a general feature of money: whatever people may intend, money has a life of its own.

In any case, sharing attitudes toward money is part of the bond in upper-class marriages, as it is between people of any group.

One woman I interviewed recalled that she and her husband, who eventually inherited many millions of dollars, spent a few years in a cramped studio apartment and refrained from even hiring a babysitter or going to the movies while her husband was in law school. Though she had $100,000 in the bank at the time, given to her by her parents, and her husband knew he would eventually inherit millions, the two had been so conditioned against touching a trust fund for any consumable item that it never occurred to them to spend a few thousand dollars of her money to make those years a little easier.

Every ethnic and class group has its own system for dealing with money in the family. Among many upper-class WASP families there is fear that children (and, especially, sons) may be spoiled by the comforts and lack of incentive easy money provides. In part, this attitude stems from anxiety over demonstrating personal worth since descendants often don't measure up to the accomplishments of their ancestors. Combine this with a fear of losing the family fortune and, with it, every basis for identity, and this results in parents who are stingy toward their children to the point of insanity. Withholding money also serves the Protestant ethic of avoiding pleasure and self-indulgence and delaying gratification, an ethic that governs middle-class WASP as well, who are also notoriously frugal.

In poor African-American families, other financial customs prevail: poverty is often so extreme that survival depends on pooling money and resources among an extended kinship network, as the anthropologist Carol Stack has described.[13] Here, as elsewhere, kinship involves an economic relationship. Poor blacks often define family not strictly in terms of blood-ties but in terms of the ever-shifting alliances of people committed to mutual aid—to pooling money, space, and child-care. In this world, a sister or brother is one who has helped you through hard times. The ethic of sharing scarce resources in order to survive is in conflict with the experience of white ethnic minorities who have been upwardly mobile in the United States: Irish, Italians, and Jews. Members of poor white ethnic groups learned that if you want to be upwardly mobile and move into the middle class you have to limit ties with the extended family. Social and economic mobility generally involves moving away from kin because it's hard to get ahead when you're encumbered by the problems and demands of needy relatives.

In a kinship system that's built on pooling resources, the individual with a little extra has a harder time refusing the claims of desperate relatives. A young professor I know who comes from a very poor Afro-American family is struggling to maintain a middle-class life-style in Manhattan on her $35,000 salary. She has to budget very carefully and can't live in the style of many of her colleagues who've inherited trust funds or have spouses who provide a second professional income. Yet, though she's barely able to pay her bills, she's considered rich by her mother and sister who live in poverty, and they can't understand why she is unable to help to support them.

Every class and ethnic group has its own customs for managing family money, though the American middle class probably has fewer clear rules. In each group, money has different meanings. Marx and Simmel were correct in observing the universal properties of money and how a market economy has affected modern relationships—for example, the ability of money to invade other values or the tendency for money to free the individual from the group. But as Viviana Zelizer has argued in her social history of "special monies,"[14] there is also variation in the cultural values, rules, and meanings that are imposed on family money.

The middle class has fewer of these shared values and rules about money precisely because the middle class is most devoted to individual mobility, which is encouraged and honored above other considerations. When money is earned rather than inherited, when identity is based on individual achievement rather than membership in a family, there are fewer compelling reasons to impose group rules on the disposition of that money. Instead, money is considered the property of the individual, and is given a more personal stamp. That is why we so often feel we know a person by his or her behavior with money. In the middle class, money is the medium for self-expression. And that is also why there is such confusion about how to share it, and so many people who feel betrayed and disappointed.

5

Money and Loss

*I*n its seeming omnipotence, money appears to provide a cushion against loss. We look to money to preserve what is loved, restore what is missing.

Old people always warn the young that someday (when it's too late) they'll recognize the value of money. Youth can afford to disparage money—who needs it when one feels that anything is possible, that the best is still ahead? Money grows in importance as the characteristics of youth—high hopes, idealism, good health, and especially, the sense of endless possibilities—diminish. As possibility fades, people turn more to preserving, insuring.

In middle age, many use money to prop open doors that are already starting to close, to keep life from narrowing. Money, representing pure possibility in its power to purchase, can provide a few extra years of choice—finance a midlife career change, a facelift, a boost to one's declining value in the sexual marketplace. In middle age, many people beautify their houses in place of the attention they once devoted to their physical appearance. As youthful attractiveness declines we create a new showpiece for ourselves. Our houses become symbols of ourselves to be noticed and admired. A house can represent many things: a parent, child, marriage, a metaphor for the self. No wonder couples remodel their houses just before they break up. It's a final effort to keep their relationship patched together.

But finally, there comes a time in life when even money can't shore up losses or buy options—indeed when options become repugnant. As Ned Rorem notes in his diaries, even the idea of possibilities becomes less appealing as people age. At first, he says, we console ourselves in times of loss with the idea that loss allows room for a new start. But eventually, losses are "just that— potholes never to be filled."[1] As people age, many lose interest in possibilities and turn their energies, instead, to conserving. Toward the end, new starts no longer have appeal. It is only the predictable and the familiar that most old people crave, and even money can't reverse this process of inversion. A woman I know thus described the last years of her father, an industrialist with many millions of dollars. In his eighties, widowed and sick, he moved from his big mansion to one of the small cottages on his estate, and then to one room of the cabin, spending his last months sitting in a particular chair, eating only one thing—asparagus, directly from the can.

Even if money can't shield us from death, it can buy a certain kind of immortality. Some old people comfort themselves by thinking of how they can control future generations by the way they arrange their legacies. The rich do live on, a bit, through the value of what they leave behind—houses, institutions, jewels, diaries, letters. The poor, having nothing of material value, vanish when they die. In a moving autobiography about returning to a small Spanish village to find his father's grave and the truth about his father's death, the novelist Jose Yglesias finally came to the end of his search with nothing but a scrap of paper on which an official had scribbled his father's dates of birth and death and the date his body was removed from its grave for disposal in an unmarked spot in a pauper's cemetery. The scrap of paper, which Yglesias folded and put in his wallet, was the only tombstone and marker his father would ever have.[2]

Because people live on in their possessions, the objects they leave behind can transmit a bit of their spirit. Sometimes an inheritance serves as a fast-frozen section of an idealized memory, a fragment made perfect in the absence of the real person. A friend of mine with argumentative, explosive parents once told me her fantasy of what her life would be like after they died. She would inherit enough money to buy an apartment overlooking Rittenhouse Square, the most peaceful view in Philadelphia. Into the apartment she would transport her mother's entire living room, which was tranquil and airy in a Japanese style—all the furniture was white, and the soft lights glowed from behind transparent screens. Initially, I was shocked at how far she'd developed this plot, but then I found it understandable. My friend is attached, perhaps too attached, to her provocative and contentious parents and still yearns for the care they never gave. Her fantasy of the inheritance and the peaceful setting it would provide promised the parental care she sought without the difficulties of the real people.

Another of my friends from a happy, supportive family had a fantasy, too, of what she would like when her mother dies. It's a gold plate commemorating the World's Fair of 1939, where her parents had spent their honeymoon. When she was a child, the plate, never used, had been displayed in a living room cabinet, and she had fancied that it was extremely valuable, "a plate fit for royalty." In wanting the plate, she wished to retain the positive side of a child's capacity to idealize. Of all her mother's possessions, she most valued the object that reminded her of the power she'd once attributed to her parents. To a small child, the plate symbolized great journeys they had taken and the things they had seen, as well as the time in their lives when they were probably happiest.

There are other ways that possessions and money bring the dead back to life. One woman thus recalls the early days of her widowhood:

> I see myself—even before the condolence letters are acknowledged—crouching in the corner of what I still call our bedroom, pawing through my files, reassuring myself over and over again about the subject that intrudes like flesh among the funeral flowers: money. Time and again, without cause, I add up the figures, as if some of them have vanished during the night. I cannot stop myself from doing it.

But there, in her husband's checkbook, she finds the evidence of a betrayal meant to remain a secret, and once again, her marriage is brought back to life:

> The seamless wall is no longer seamless. Water can seep through this chink. A few minutes ago, I was a widow, but suddenly I am transformed to a wife again, an outraged wife at that.[3]

In one family I know of, the parents always sought to control what life presented to them—including death—with money. One of their grown sons, after a lifetime of slavish devotion to his parents, shocked everyone by moving to another state, marrying a Catholic woman (his parents are ardently Jewish), and getting an unlisted phone number. When he died unexpectedly at forty, his widow called her husband's father to tell him the news. Hearing that his son had died and that he was to be cremated according to his deathbed instructions, the father offered his daughter-in-law (whom he knew to be in desperate financial need) several thousand dollars if she would return the body so that his son might have a proper Jewish burial in the family plot. When his daughter-in-law refused, the father withdrew his money offer.

Children, too, use money to contest the power of death or loss. And, like adults, they often seek possessions when they're most overwhelmed by loss. One of the most memorable scenes in a PBS series on American families focused on a thirteen-year-old boy who had just learned that his parents were going to divorce. Sitting on his bed, he responded to the news by recounting how much money each relative had given him for his bar mitzvah.

The crushing sense of loss that most of us experience, one way or another in childhood, becomes embedded in the projects of adulthood. One of the greatest losses of childhood is the realization that a parent is weak or unhappy. Children want to rescue their parents not only from death but from failure. Even young children intuit their parents' disappointments and sadness, and many of us spend our adult lives in an unconscious quest to symbolically rescue a parent or avoid their fate. Often, people see money as the means for restoring the broken portions of their parents' lives.

During adolescence, a man I know had witnessed his father go through a long period of depression during which he made poor business decisions and lost the considerable family fortune amassed by the boy's grandparents. The son has devoted his life to making a great deal of money, not because he craves possessions but because it became his unconscious mission to restore his father and his family to the security and strength he had imagined they had as a child, before his father's illness.

A woman I know, a professor of literature, is married to a wealthy man who owns a chain of clothing stores. For twenty years, Carol Rossi has complained that her husband bores her, that he has no interest in books or ideas or the aspects of life that she values. Partly out of fear of looking stupid, her husband refuses to read a book. He deals with his wife's contempt by displaying his own contempt for writers, artists, and intellectuals.

At times, Carol has thought of leaving her husband, but she's always stopped by an irrational image of sinking into abject poverty if she does. Her fear is irrational because any lawyer would tell her that she'd take at least a few million dollars away from the marriage. Knowing that she doesn't love him, her husband plays on her fears of poverty in order to control her and bind her to the marriage. "You won't be able to afford to *heat* this house if we get divorced," he threatens her, whenever she starts to talk about a divorce and dividing their houses and property.

Searching her soul for why she married him, Carol Rossi would say it was primarily the attraction to security. As a child, she had been neglected and fended for herself in a chaotic, sloppy household. In her mother's eyes, her father, an Italian immigrant, had never succeeded, and she treated him like a dirty, embarrassing peasant. Besides money, Carol's husband offered her the stability and order she missed in childhood, including big beautiful houses with live-in servants. When she thinks of divorce, she always imagines being left without a nice, clean home.

Rossi's marriage expresses the opposing impulses from her childhood: marrying a rich, orderly, attentive (in fact, controlling) man was not only a way to compensate for the neglect of her childhood but, unconsciously, a way to defend her father against her mother—here is a man who can not be accused of being a failure or a dirty peasant. On the other hand, echoes of her mother's contempt for her father creep into Carol's own attitude when she looks down on her husband for his disinterest in literature and the arts. And though Carol's husband comes from a rich and well-educated family, he displays an obsequious manner whenever he's around the wealthy WASPs they entertain. This weakness, too, reignites painful memories in Carol about her father. In her marriage, she has restaged her parent's conflict and her place within it: at once, enacting an identification with her mother, a defense of her father, and an attempt to find what she'd been denied in childhood.

One of the greatest motivations in life is to escape the fate of one's parents, even as we instinctively veer toward it, like a homing pigeon. Rossi assumed that her father was a failure in her mother's eyes because he didn't earn enough money, and that marrying a man with money would be her way out of that trap. But the unconscious compulsion to reenact the traumas of childhood has a driving force that even money can't alter. How many people think they've avoided the problem of their parents' marriage, only to discover that they've reproduced the marriage using very different material? When it comes to the compulsion of repetition, money merely embellishes the story or provides a larger stage for acting out familiar dramas. It's ironic that although money has many powers, it does not have the power to spring us from self-defeating plots. One kind of situation I think of involves a familiar drama, the rescue of the beloved.

There are countless myths and stories about ambitious men who marry up, but less has been written about women who do, perhaps because traditionally we've had few stories about heroines seeking their fortunes. In serious and popular fiction, when a talented and ambitious woman has married into a higher class, she's typically had the chance because the man was seriously damaged in some way. Among the best known of these fictional heroines are Charlotte Bronte's Jane Eyre and Daphne DuMaurier's Rebecca. In both cases, the power their lovers possess from being male and rich is offset by serious emotional or physical wounds. In this matter, life seems to imitate fiction. In the few real-life situations I've known where a woman married into a higher class, she married a man viewed as a failure, even by his own family. Oddly, the weakness of the man seems to be part of the appeal; it evens things out. Because of the weakness, the woman—otherwise subordinate by sex and background—is able to take charge.

An actual case that comes to mind concerns a woman I have named Ann Gardner. She grew up in a middle-class Jewish family but always thought she deserved to be rich. Her family would indeed have been wealthier had it not been for the fact that her mother's manic-depressive illness drained the family resources, because she needed extensive psychiatric care and long rest periods in expensive sanitariums. Even so, Ann attended private schools and an Ivy League university, always choosing for friends people who came from privileged backgrounds. When she was twenty-five she met and soon after married a man from an old-money WASP family. He'd grown up in a beautiful house on a hill near Princeton, New Jersey, surrounded by gardens, vistas, and stables for the horses. His father was a towering, intimidating, widely admired figure who was president of an important manufacturing plant in New Jersey.

On weekends and holidays, Ann, her husband, and their son would leave their small Manhattan apartment to visit his parents at their mansion. Here they could live like junior royalty for the weekend, with all kinds of help at their service. At Christmas, it was, as she described it, a child's dream come true—the entire house was decorated with cloves and glass angels.

This would have been a Cinderella story except for the fact that Ann's husband was extremely vulnerable. Even before they married, Ann knew he suffered from serious depressions because he had been hospitalized during their courtship. Clearly, she had fallen in love with the family as much as with the son. Like many "orphans" in myths and in real life, she had sought a strong, aristocratic family to make up for the care missing in her childhood. In fact, she was aware that her husband's illness was probably part of the attraction: "It seemed very romantic at the time— my mother was manic-depressive, so I had lived with this. Freud says we repeat the experiences of childhood in the hope that we can master them, but often we don't. You would think we'd run in the opposite direction."

Ann's husband always felt like a failure in his father's eyes and was, in fact, regarded as one. Not surprisingly, he had a total breakdown at the age of forty after his parents died and their big house had been sold and destroyed to make room for an ugly housing development. Though he was now rich and doing fairly well at work, Ann's husband sank into an extreme depression from which he never recovered. After trying to kill himself, he turned into a zombie as a result of his depression and the shock treatments and drugs he takes for it. During the past eight years, he's been in and out of one of New York's most expensive psychiatric hospitals, a tragic and guilty way of spending his inheritance.

For a year after the suicide attempt, Ann stayed in the marriage, tending to her husband's sickness. "Did you take your pills?" she would have to ask every day. When he showed no signs of improving she divorced him, justifying the abandonment on the grounds that she had to protect herself so her son would have one sane parent. Many of their friends disapproved, especially their lawyer (her husband's college roommate), who thought she had no right to keep half the properties they had bought with his inheritance. At the time of the purchases, Ann had insisted that they be placed in both names, so she was legally, if not morally, entitled to them. "I told [the lawyer] Richard might not have inherited the money without me. I kept him functioning. And it was my idea to buy the apartment, which has quintupled in value."

The obvious accusation is that she married not for love but for money. Her husband certainly feared she had, and she told me she wasn't sure herself. Yet what does it mean, to marry for money? Like "marrying for love" the concept covers a range of motives.

Though money and social mobility figured largely in Ann's love for her husband, it would be too simple to say she married him only for his money. Though his illness was part of his attraction for her, clearly Ann would not have married Richard Gardner if he were merely a poor depressed man. His background and his need to be rescued had combined to provide the proper family romance. For her husband, Richard, marrying a Jewish woman had been an act of rebellion against his parents. "Marrying down" (from his parents' point of view) was also a way of trading on his money and family for what he lacked in himself.

I tell this story because it illustrates how closely money may be woven into what psychologists regard as Oedipal fantasies. In gothic novels like *Jane Eyre, Rebecca,* and the thousands of modern romances they have inspired, the heroine invariably falls in love with a man with a big house, a man who must be rescued from entrapment to his first wife. No doubt, these stories appeal, in part, to Oedipal wishes—the big house representing the house of one's childhood, the man in need of rescue representing one's father.

Freud believed that rescue fantasies derived from the beliefs we develop in childhood to deal with our inability to compete successfully against one parent for the love of the other. Freud argued that little boys could never accept the idea that their mothers *wanted* to have sex with their fathers. They preferred to believe that their mothers, and subsequent love objects modeled on their mothers, were trapped against their will by their husbands and therefore were in need of rescue.[4] The same unconscious motivation may be read into Gothic romances in which young heroines must rescue men who are trapped in unhappy marriages with older women: Freud's insight would suggest they are repeating their childhood desire to liberate their fathers from their mothers.

In Ann Gardner's case, the somewhat universal wish to rescue her father (and, therefore, later lovers) was deepened by the special circumstances of her family life. Because her mother was sick and incompetent, and frequently living away from home, as a child Ann took over much of her mother's role in relation to her father. While her mother was hospitalized with depression, Ann was the woman of the house, her father's comfort and partner. This early "rescue" of her father probably set the stage for her subsequent attraction to a man who needed to be rescued.

There is often a psychological connection[5] between a strong fixation on social mobility and unconscious Oedipal yearnings. People who are Oedipally fixated are characteristically attracted to doomed, impossible, or tragic relationships. People who are obsessed with mobility are also emotionally drawn to what is out of reach. There is also a similarity between the psychological dynamics of doomed romantic love and social climbing. Social climbers, like unrequited lovers,[6] usually pick for the object of their desire the very person who wants nothing to do with them and project onto that person qualities that aren't really there. Like lovers, social climbers are often touchingly superior to those they pursue. And like lovers, they suffer from rejection but are even more devastated by the loss of their illusions, for they have tied their own self-worth to the projected stature of their idol.

Obviously, Ann Gardner was attracted to her husband's background and money, and these figured largely in her love for the man, but attraction to money is more than cold calculation. When people fall in love with money there are intervening fantasies. In Ann's case, the money and the big, beautiful house provided an illusion of warmth, protection, nurture, stability, solidity—the happy, comfortable family she never had, the idealized parents she was still looking for.

I thought of Ann Gardner when I watched the popular BBC production of Evelyn Waugh's novel *Brideshead Revisited*. The story opens during World War II when Charles Ryder, a disillusioned officer in the British army, is recalled by chance to Brideshead, the ancestral estate of the Marchmains, a noble British family. Deserted by its owners during the war, the once magnificent palace is now in ruins. Ryder recalls the happier times of his youth at Brideshead, the only time in his life he had known love. A kind of orphan—his mother died young, and he could make no human connection with his eccentric father—Ryder had found at Brideshead "a brief spell of what I had never known, a happy childhood."[7] Though he's expelled from the house "like a schoolboy" by Lady Marchmain, he knows that he has left behind a part of himself and that "wherever I went afterwards I should feel the lack of it, and search for it hopelessly, as ghosts are said to do."[8] In fact, he makes a career of painting beautiful houses slated for destruction. He is ruled by nostalgia and a pervasive sense of loss.

In the television production, Ryder's love for the ancestral estate is the central theme: the musical love theme swells whenever the house appears in the background, glittering through the mist, like a temple. Like many houses, it's a shelter for memory, for what can be preserved from the ruins of the past. "My theme is memory," says Ryder. "These memories, which are my life—for we possess nothing certainly except the past—were always with me."[9] Beneath all his social and romantic aspirations, he is drawn to the house; one never relinquishes the wish to have had a happy childhood. But in *Brideshead*, even money can't rescue the house or its occupants from the destruction that time imposes. The notion that wealth can preserve against loss turns out to be an illusion.

Which brings me back to Ann Gardner. Like the hero of *Brideshead Revisited* she fell in love with the great house and its owners in the hope that money could restore what she lost in childhood. It was only when she talked of the impotence of money to restore her husband's sanity that she displayed any sadness for his condition: "You're brought up to think if you really go to the top men—it can be fixed. There was no limit on money, or resources, or knowledge, we could buy the best specialists. I figured we must be able to fix this—but it couldn't be fixed."

6

—•—

Lesser Trumps

*I*n *The Art of the Deal*, published in 1987, Donald Trump disclosed some of the tricks of his trade, his "trump cards," in the art of beating rivals and winning in the deal. They boil down to some simple principles: think big, don't take risks, shift the burden of risk to someone else's shoulders, maximize options, don't get too attached to any particular deal, never let your rival smell blood, make your opponent need you, use leverage. In some ways, Trump's advice reminds me of the teenage lessons my older sister used to give me in the art of getting a boy to love you: make him jealous, play the field, always let him know you're capable of walking out the door.

Do the same principles apply in love as in business? If the best sellers are any indication, people like to think that love is different, that love is not a zero-sum game (in which a gain for one side entails a loss for the other), and everyone can come out ahead. But can people who live and breathe to make the best deal at the office stop themselves from playing hardball at home?

Although Donald Trump devoted a chapter to each of his great deals, he didn't even hint at his most valuable contract—the nuptial agreement with his wife Ivana, updated three times during their thirteen year marriage to ensure the agreement was not just ironclad but "steel wrapped." Although Ivana is depicted in *The Art of the Deal* as a smart businesswoman in her own right, it was all over the press in 1990, when Donald asked for a divorce, that he had managed to make his wife sign away her "equitable" (according to New York State law) half-share of the billions of dollars the Trumps had earned during their marriage. According to news

65

reports about the last agreement, reportedly signed on Christmas Eve 1987, Ivana was to get less than 1 percent of the property.

The deal for Ivana, which was portrayed by the media as shocking, illustrates one of my own laws of money: many people obsessed with outwitting rivals in business relate to their own spouses in exactly the same way. How could they not? As Trump himself has pointed out, smart businesspeople never leave their flanks uncovered. And who would know your points of vulnerability better than your spouse?

Most of the wheeler-dealers I've known have had interesting things to say about their divorces. In almost every case, they approached their divorce with the same gamesmanship they bring to business. Some even relished this ultimate contest with their spouse. One who comes to mind is a wealthy accountant who operated according to Trump's principles years before the publication of *The Art of the Deal.*

George Papadopoulos is one of the most successful accountants in the Midwest. His business occupies a vast suite in the most expensive and glamorous office building in Chicago. He employs thirty accountants, and farms out work to many more. He is acutely concerned with his image and so has lunch every single weekday at the same restaurant, the most expensive in town, because he thinks it's important to be seen there.

Originally, I'd arranged to meet Papadopoulos to talk about the special problems of family-owned businesses, but not ten minutes into our conversation, he started to vent his feelings about his current divorce. He preceded this with his philosophy of money:

> Money is everything. It's a reflection of your abilities and your capacities. . . . There are two important reasons for having money. One is that if you have money you can have everything you want. The second is that money shows what you're worth.
>
> Let me give you a quotable quote. Money is a means of keeping score—after a certain point, after you have everything you want. There are three levels to money. On an after-tax basis, if you're earning up to three hundred thousand bucks, you're making a living. After that, you're getting into accumulation. A stage above that is the scorekeeping stage. It starts at a couple of million bucks. If a

person has more than that in real money—I don't mean
equity in a company or a house that you can't spend—but a
liquid net worth of two to three million dollars, it's not ac-
cumulation that counts, but keeping score.

I've had a lengthy discussion with my children about this.
They live in Evanston, and what do kids talk about? He has
sixty thousand dollars worth of cars in his driveway, he has
eighty-two thousand dollars in his driveway. In fact, here's
another quotable quote. In the suburbs, you know how you
can tell a successful person? Not by the car he drives, but
by the *second* car. That's the clue. If you live in an affluent
community everyone has a Cadillac or a Mercedes. What
the hell's the difference? But—the truly affluent guy is the
one who has two Mercedes or a Mercedes and a Cadillac or
a Mercedes and a Corvette. Very interesting. Think about
it. It's the second car that controls, not the first.

Like Trump, Papadopoulos attributes his wealth to his skills at
knowing how to manipulate people. When he started his business,
he borrowed almost $1 million to put his offices in the most ex-
pensive building in Chicago. Then he used "reverse psychology":

I don't publicize who my clients are—I act wealthier than
my clients. It was my game. I've created an exclusive club
and no one knows who's in it. I have people come to my
office and I interview them to see if I want them to be my
client, rather than pitching myself to them. I've had stock-
brokers say, "Do I pass? Do you want me for a client?"

At the moment, Papadopoulos's biggest challenge is his divorce.
After she caught him in bed with another woman, his wife asked
for a divorce, and now they're preparing to slug it out in court.
Unlike Trump, Papadopoulos didn't have a prenuptial agreement
in his first marriage, but he would never marry again without one.

I met my wife when we were kids. My wife came into the
marriage with a bad set of teeth and a Chevrolet Corvair.
As you grow older, you start to go in different directions,
and then, if you start to get successful, the husband typically thinks, what if? what if? what if? what if? There's a

level of self-defense on the part of the husband—not telling his wife what's going on. If I got married again there would be a business contract. If you have a contract that says if we separate you get a quarter of a million bucks, if I die you're the beneficiary of a million dollar policy and that's it, everything else goes to my kids, then I've got no fear of telling her anything. It doesn't make a difference.

I ask Papadopoulos, wouldn't a woman be angry, knowing that you didn't want her to get more? He replies:

That's the best story of all. A woman marries a man. They sign an antenuptial agreement. He represents his net worth to be two million and says to her, look, if I die or we get divorced you get a quarter of a million bucks. She looks and says, yeah, it's fair, and signs the agreement. The old boy dies three years later and they admit his will to probate and he's not worth two million bucks, he's worth ten million bucks. She sues for fraud. She can get angry all she wants. As long as the representations made at the time are correct, it's a binding agreement. She can get angry all she wants. I truly think it makes for a better relationship. If it's spelled out, you can afford to be free and open and do what you want.

Papadopoulos has his rough edges, but the more I think about what he says, the more I agree. Few people who have passed their twenties or lived through a divorce are so naive they don't occasionally ask "what if?", though few have the confidence to press for the divorce agreement in advance. And when Papadopoulos admits that it wouldn't bother him if his second wife resented the contract as long as he was protected, he strikes me as more perceptive than insensitive. The pain and anger of a partner who feels betrayed have curiously little impact on a deal-maker who's glad that he protected himself. Papadopoulos's sentiments are echoed in the confession of a young Wall Street bond trader who misled his favorite client into making a bad deal that cost the client $60,000. As Michael Lewis tells the story, when he phoned his client with the bad news, all he heard was an agonized noise and the sound of hyperventilation:

And you want to know how I felt? I should have felt guilty, of course, but guilt was not the first identifiable sensation to emerge from my exploding brain. Relief was. I had told him the news. He was shouting and moaning. And that was it. That was all he could do. Shout and moan. That was the beauty of being a middleman, which I did not appreciate until that moment. The customer suffered. I didn't. He wasn't going to kill me. He wasn't even going to sue me. I wasn't going to lose *my* job. On the contrary, I was a minor hero at Salomon for dumping a sixty-thousand-dollar loss into someone else's pocket.

There was a convenient way of looking at this situation. My customer did not like the loss, but it was just as much his own fault as mine. The law of the bond market is: caveat emptor. That's Latin for "buyer beware."[1]

Of course, the feelings are far more complicated in marriage. In Papadopoulos's story of his marriage, boasting, anger, and self-pity all come together; in his household, he can't maintain the image of the successful businessman. His deepest hurt is that no one in his family has recognized or appreciated him for the amount of money he's earned, even though everywhere else money is the measure of a man's value. No wonder so many men put more effort into making money than making their relationships work—it's easier to succeed at making money. With his wife, Papadopoulos can't win:

I spent a quarter of a million dollars in the last two years of my marriage to keep the marriage together. It just didn't make a damn bit of difference. She wanted to redo the house—I spent a hundred fifty thousand dollars redoing the master bedroom. She didn't like the house in the Bahamas [where Papadopoulos spends five days every month] so I built her a new house. April 16, it's a zoo here, and she plans a three-week trip to Europe. Can you imagine, dragging the kids and a hundred pounds of cameras after going through hell working weekends in tax season?

My middle son asked me, would I do anything differently if I had it all to do again? I said to him, you think I wouldn't have gone out with other women? That's not true. What about what she did to me? For Mother's Day, she'll spend fifty dollars on a gift for my mother and three hundred fifty dollars for her mother. That kind of thing. And our parents are friendly, so they compare gifts. I said to my son, you know what I would have done differently? When I started this firm, for the first nine months I didn't draw a salary. During that time my kids went to camp and my wife took three trips—one to Las Vegas and two to the Bahamas. That fall we took the kids to New England. We didn't have the money but she didn't give a damn. She was depressed that year, so she bought herself two rings—one diamond and one emerald. I had my first hundred thousand dollar deal, and there was a problem in the deal. I had to cancel a trip to the Bahamas to finish the deal and she went crazy, and that deal has led to two-and-a-half million dollars in fees in the last two years.

I told my son what I did wrong was not letting the entire family participate in the building of the business. Their mother did whatever she wanted—she lived like a queen at the country club—I had to stay in the country club because I had to have the image that I had the money. But she didn't have to have diamond rings and a housekeeper and the kids didn't have to go to camp. . . . If she had worked with me and done without certain things, she would have had an appreciation for what all this meant. No one in our family has any appreciation for what I've created. The outside world understands what I've done. To my family, I just went from one job to another job, and this one is more lucrative than the first.

A year after I started the firm I thought, you know something—I've killed myself. Everyone had what they wanted but me. So I went and bought a car. A toy. I have an Avanti. I haven't heard the end of that yet from my wife and I worked it out tax-wise so it cost me nothing. "I can't believe you bought that car," she told me. Then I bought a Mississippi river barge. I paid thirty-three thousand dollars and saved sixty thousand dollars in taxes. "Well, if you bought yourself a barge, I want a ring." "What are you talking about?" I said. "It's a tax shelter. I'll buy you anything you want if you can work it out as a tax shelter."

Now that he's divorcing, Papadopoulos's love of a contest, and his need to reduce anxiety about what his wife might do to him provide the fuel for his divorce preparations. He assures himself that he is in total control:

I feel the only way I can have a good relationship with my children is to go to court. I can't deal with that woman—she won't bargain or negotiate. My problem is that I've been involved with too many divorce situations as an accountant. The stuff I've done you wouldn't believe. I have driven husbands and wives up the wall with some of the tricks I've pulled—legitimately. My wife has the children convinced that nobody could beat me. She went to the best lawyer before, and I beat him. If I negotiate with her and we settle, she'll convince the children that I browbeat her, that I'm unfair. But I feel psychologically that if the judge orders something, I can turn to my children and say, look, there's an independent person. The children have respect for our judicial and political system because I taught them to respect it. If I have an independent person say something, that's the law, and they will accept that. She has a lawyer, and I have a lawyer, and the two argued and this is what they agreed upon. So it's very important for a judge to rule because she will convince them that I'm so powerful.

In the next moment, Papadopoulos can't resist the urge to remind me how powerful he is:

It took her ten months to get an accountant who would take the case on. All the large firms here have relations with me because we delegate out work and they work for me. And I do a lot of lecturing. They say, what am I crazy, going against him? She finally got one guy. He's got an office and a secretary and one associate in a space this big (he gestures to half the space in his personal office). They have a piece of glass separating each person—that's their office.

He's the guy who took her case on. He's about sixty-four and no one's ever heard of him.

I'm orchestrating the whole thing from A to Z. I put together the affidavits. My lawyer just takes the stuff and retypes it. I have torn apart every single document she sends, and I do it all myself. That's not to say my legal bills haven't gone to thirty-five thousand dollars already.

He pulls out stacks of paper and explains that to answer just the first set of interrogatories from his wife he will have to copy fifteen thousand pieces of paper and it will take sixty man hours to do the job. He smiles at her new interest in his business. "When we were married, my wife only wanted to know how much she could spend. She didn't want to know where it came from, what I owed, what I was doing. Then she wanted to know nothing."

Big dealers like Papadopoulos don't hesitate to claim that money is the measure of a man's worth. It takes unusual insight to resist this self-serving assumption when you've earned a fortune. In his brilliant description of learning to swim with the sharks at Salomon Brothers before the stock crash of 1987, Michael Lewis captures how powerfully money becomes the measure of worth, particularly in the world of money. He recalls that on bonus day, at the end of December, each of the younger traders would be summoned, one by one, into a meeting with the boss to hear the judgment they'd been waiting for:

> On January 1, 1987, 1986 would be erased from memory
> except for a single number: the amount of money you
> were paid. That number was the final summing up. Imag-
> ine being told you will meet with the divine Creator in a
> year's time to be told your worth as a human being.[2]

According to Lewis, the wildness of pre–October 1987 Wall Street was a modern gold rush, when sudden windfalls from the new bond market turned twenty-four-year-olds like himself into instant millionaires and transformed their managers into world-class financial celebrities:

> I assumed the strange behavior of our managers was sim-
> ply a response to having had a pile of loot dropped into

their laps. . . . There they were, modest men, living off other people's scraps, when all of a sudden the big stuffed bird was handed to them. They were doing nothing more than what they had always done, yet overnight glory was thrust upon them. Their incomes had changed, and with it their lives. Imagine.

If you are a self-possessed man with a healthy sense of detachment from your bank account and someone writes you a check for tens of millions of dollars, you probably behave as if you have won a sweepstakes, kicking your feet in the air and laughing yourself to sleep at night at the miracle of your good fortune. But if your sense of self-worth is morbidly wrapped up in your financial success, you probably believe you deserve everything you get. You take it as a reflection of something grand inside you. You acquire *gravitas* and project it like a cologne.[3]

Michael Lewis is one of the few contemporary authors writing about dealing and hustling who isn't taken in by the romance of money. Although the Trumps and the Papadopouloses regard their fortunes as measures of their talent, Lewis points out that many make fortunes because they're in the right place at the right time:

The biggest myth about bond traders, and therefore the greatest misunderstanding about the unprecedented prosperity on Wall Street in the 1980's, are that they make their money by taking large risks. A few do. And all traders take small risks. But most traders act simply as toll takers. The source of their fortune has been nicely summarized by Kurt Vonnegut (who, oddly, was describing lawyers): "There is a magic moment, during which a man has surrendered a treasure, and during which the man who is about to receive it has not yet done so. An alert lawyer [read bond trader] will make that moment his own, possessing the treasure for a magic microsecond, taking a little of it, passing it on."

In other words, Salomon carved a tiny fraction out of each financial transaction. This adds up.[4]

Actually, this view is very close to Trump's advice, except that Trump convinces himself that he's raised the level of deal making so high that it's been transformed into an "'art'": "Deals are my art form. Other people paint beautifully on canvas or write wonderful poetry. I like making deals."[5]

Do people really enjoy outsmarting their loved ones, too? Zick Rubin, a psychologist, has written insightfully about his own tendency to keep count, even with his eight-year-old son. At the start of a two-and-a-half week summer vacation, Rubin and his little boy visited the public library and stocked up on reading supplies. His son chose seven child-length biographies, while Rubin picked a weighty social history. Over the vacation, father and son worked their ways through the volumes:

> As it turned out, we weren't just reading. We were also keeping count. I would periodically ask Elihu how many of his books he had read, and he would periodically ask me what page I was on. By the end of the weekend, I was proudly telling my wife that Elihu had read six of his books, and Elihu was bragging to his friends about the huge tome that I was reading. After Elihu had finished all seven books, he enlisted my help in computing the total number of pages he had read. They added up to 409, and he was only slightly disappointed to note that this total was less than the 500-odd pages that I had completed. I couldn't resist pointing out that some of the pages he was counting contained pictures, while mine were all words.[6]

Is keeping count a distinctly male preoccupation? Rubin seems to think so, and argues that men's involvement with number games stems from their well-known obsession with individual achievement and tabulating their accomplishments to measure and demonstrate their masculinity. Noticing that his son does not engage in score-keeping with his mother, Rubin concludes this is a bit of masculinity that men pass on to their sons. I'm not so sure that women don't count, although maybe we do it more surreptitiously.

Perhaps everyone counts, but men do seem more concerned about not being "suckered" in a deal. For many, in every human encounter there's a winner and a loser, and to be the loser is unbearable. I've seen many rich men devote inordinate attention to ensure even the pettiest of financial victories, as if their sense of pride couldn't stand being taken advantage of. One man I know who earns millions every year is always on the lookout for anyone who might be trying to cheat him of pennies, and saving a dollar can bring him the same pleasure as pulling off a big deal. During one vacation in Mexico with his wife that cost him $10,000, he brooded every morning about having to pay a dollar-fifty for a small glass of orange juice. He was able to relax and enjoy himself only after he figured out a way to buy his own quart of juice and brazenly pour from it at the hotel breakfast table. For men like this, every penny saved represents a defense against assault and assures the intactness of their masculinity.

Another man I know earns a good living as a commercial film-maker, but he still takes great pleasure in cheating customers out of a few dollars, for example, by charging them for equipment he's really buying for himself. His philosophy is, "If they're fools, let them pay for it." Sometimes, while discussing a project with a client, he finds himself thinking about how much money he's making that day. Thinking about the money pacifies him, he claims, and distracts him from feeling anxious. It helps fend off feelings of helplessness because when he calculates his earnings he knows there's a concrete gain that gives him a sense of control. Having enough money means he won't be at the mercy of his feelings.

Often, when he can't sleep at night, he'll get up and pay bills. This reassures him that he has power and that he's in control. He still has the fantasy that he'll end up poor, helpless, and beaten, like his parents, and when he goes through poor neighborhoods, the fear overtakes him. He explains his drive to take advantage as his revenge for childhood neglect.

Women, too, are reassured by knowing they have taken advantage. One wealthy businesswoman I know gets the greatest pleasure from squeezing every penny out of a deal. A purchase is no fun for many people unless they've gotten a great bargain. They enjoy the successful bargaining more than they enjoy the object. I know several women who can't bear to buy a dress unless it's been marked down at least 50 percent. While bargain hunting has a less combative quality than outsmarting a rival in a deal, they may both have their origins in the need to get even or come out ahead.

Of course, department stores manipulate people like this by doubling the ticket price so they can mark it down.

I began by asking whether people who live and breathe to get the best deal ever stop themselves when it comes to their families. A few can—I know some merciless dealers who regard their spouses as trusted allies and coconspirators in their battles with the world outside the family. But, on the whole, people who are driven to win also drive a hard bargain at home. It's in their character. Everything is a power issue for them, and they always need to gain control or get the other person to capitulate. As the accountant Papadopoulos admitted, when you're a dealer, knowing you're in control is ultimately more important than how the other person feels. Yet dealers also pay a price for bringing their loved ones to their knees.

One woman, writing about her prenuptial agreement in which she agreed to a ridiculously low $25,000 parting fee should she and her rich Hollywood producer husband divorce, believes it spoiled their relationship: "It ruined the whole marriage because it gave one party the upper hand. It fosters fear and insecurity. I was quite dispensable. I could leave without making a dent in his life."[7]

When people are too successful in driving a hard bargain, they pay a price by forcing the other either into insecurity or into covert defenses. I've heard building contractors say that when clients use competitive offers to make them bid too low, they usually strike back by cutting corners on material or workmanship in ways their clients will never discover. They have no choice. The same is true in intimate relationships. Viviana Zelizer describes how earlier generations of wives who had no money of their own turned to underground strategies like padding domestic bills or picking their husbands' pockets.[8] At the extreme, partners who have walked into a bad deal may be forced to become spies in their own homes. In a recent newspaper column on managing money, financial advisor Jane Bryant Quinn presented the dilemma of one of her readers, a college professor who had been married for thirty-eight years: "I am in trouble. I have reason to believe that my husband is seeing another woman. I have never been interested much in our financial affairs. But I know I need to protect myself. What should I do?"

Quinn warns her readers that they should never get into this position in the first place, because married women can't afford not to have their "hands on the money." Now this woman has no choice, says Quinn, but to snoop around, developing a "cover story" that allows her to assemble all her husband's financial information. She provides some lessons in detection (get old copies of joint income tax returns and joint credit histories) and advises, "If you never before opened your husband's or wife's top desk drawer, now is the time to start."[9]

Who would want to live with a partner who snoops in their drawers, goes through their pockets, and secretly cuts corners? But this is what dealers often bring upon themselves when they drive unreasonable bargains at home. There's probably more of this than we'd like to acknowledge. At home, as in the political world, the exercise of oppressive power breeds guerilla warfare or passive aggression.

Fortunately, most people don't want to bully their loved ones or bring them to their knees, and there's even a brighter side to learning how to bargain and making deals at home. As any good shopper knows, honest bargaining can be great fun, and sometimes everyone comes out with a deal they like. Popular psychology has been trying to make this point and convince us there are win-win deals. With the increased use of contracts and negotiations in love relationships, we're all going to have to learn how to bargain constructively.

The problem is, in business what gives buyers power is their ability to walk away from the deal and take their money elsewhere. In the family, people exercise emotional or sexual withdrawal to get what they want, but it's not so easy to walk out the door. And some of the terms that hard bargainers insist on are both intolerable and nonnegotiable.

I know a few men, for example, who married their second wives on the absolute condition that there would be no children. They already had children, and, in any case, would not bend on this point. In every case the women agreed, but many later found they couldn't live with this bargain. Usually the women agreed because they had no choice and figured their husbands might eventually come around. In only one instance have I seen the man give in to make his wife happy. More often, for the women, it's a source of never-ending disappointment, which seems to grow rather than diminish. In one case, a woman I know did leave a husband she dearly loved because she discovered as she approached forty that she had made a deal she couldn't sustain. Within a year she was remarried and pregnant, and to this day the husband she left feels betrayed because the terms had been clear when they married.

There will always be some nonnegotiable terms that make it hard to bargain in love and marriage. Unlike doing business, it's usually not possible to walk away and buy elsewhere, but families could still learn a few tricks from the business world. In business, we bargain and make deals all the time; mostly, it works out for everyone. In my current job as chairperson of an academic department I have no power and a lot of responsibility. Several times a week I have to think of ways to get other people (the faculty) to do things they don't want to do, like serve on committees. Because I have little power and can exercise it only rarely, most of the time I have to think of ways to make a deal. Usually, I can think of something my colleagues want (freedom from another responsibility, for example) or I ask them what they want that's in my power to give and we bargain until we strike a deal. Almost all the time, this works and everyone's happy.

One of the most entertaining assignments I give to my students of social interaction is to have them go into a store where bargaining isn't the custom and have them try to strike an advantageous deal. Students are always shocked to discover that you can negotiate successfully almost everywhere—even in places like a department store or an airline ticket counter, where most customers wouldn't dream of offering anything but the stated price. In fact, many salespeople and storeowners are surprisingly accommodating and flexible. They'll often find a mutually satisfying and honest way to give customers what they want. I've had department store salespeople mark down nonsale items if they're wrinkled or about to go on sale, and airline representatives give advance-purchase discounts even when I'm buying a ticket for the next flight. I've also had airline representatives allow me to change the dates of travel on supposedly nonchangeable tickets. They have discretion to bend the rules. If you're pleasant and ask them for help, they'll often give you a break, especially if they have empty seats they'd like to fill.

It's odd we can't negotiate with this kind of ease in the family, where one would think there's greater motivation to make one another happy. Perhaps it's because, in love, we tend to focus too much on the deals our partners refuse to make, and thus forget about all the other possibilities. There is a little Trump and Papadopoulos in most of us, though thankfully, few of us are so oriented to control that we turn our loved ones into spies or adversaries. Many of us could profit by doing more good-humored bargaining at home.

Children are always making deals or trades with one another. They're not embarrassed to state what they want and to negotiate for it. It's a shame many adults have forgotten how to do this comfortably. If family members could say to one another, "I'll give you this if you give me that," or "I'll truly forgive you for this if you really forgive me for that," we might make our partnerships more satisfying.

7

·

Spenders and Payers

*A*nyone who has ever supported another adult financially, be it a grown child or a spouse who earns less, knows the mixed feelings this can elicit. At best, there is pleasure in giving something to one you love; at worst, there is the dreadful suspicion of not being loved but rather being used and exploited. For many of us there is also the comfort of knowing one exercises a little power over the recipients—they owe us something, and they can never leave as long as they need us to pay.

A man I know tells his wife, "You'll never leave me, because if you do, you won't be able to afford to keep up this house." I wonder why he stays married if he feels so unloved. But men are more comfortable than women with the idea of being motivated or ruled by money, and the thought of using it to insure love does not threaten their sense of masculinity.

Until recently, most women I know who outearn their husbands have had a harder time of it. Even when the women could forgive their husbands for being financially dependent, they've found that their sexual relationship suffered. Men seem to lose their desire for wives who earn more, or to need another lover to make them feel independent or to boost their power in the marriage.

Now that we're exploring new gender arrangements, it's becoming more common for women to marry younger men and men who earn less. Undoubtedly these modern combinations will generate fewer personal and sexual problems when they become less exceptional. But will financial domination ever be separable from power? When women have more money and status than their partners, won't they act like men?

There's some evidence that women are less likely to use money for control. In their study of American couples,[1] sociologists Philip Blumstein and Pepper Schwartz found that only lesbian couples maintained domestic equality when there were significant earning disparities. I've also observed that women are less likely than men to expect their partners to be personally accommodating because they earn less. But that's only true as long as they believe the relationship is satisfying. As soon as these women recognize their anger or disappointment with a partner, financial control allows them to reverse the traditional roles and act like "men."

In fact, a lot of what we define as "masculine" or "feminine" is actually behavior that more precisely stems from being financially dominant or dependent. Because women usually earn less than their husbands, it's easy to mistake the infantilizing effects of financial dependence for something deeper in the feminine psyche. Actually, when men are financially dependent, they act exactly like "'women."

A woman I know, a high-school teacher, has been the solitary wage earner in her family for the past twenty years. Her husband has always stayed home and done the cooking and cleaning for the couple and their three daughters, though now that the youngest is in high school, he has less of an excuse for not getting a job. After putting up with this arrangement for years, the wife surprised even herself by acquiring a lover with whom she spends every night. For the past year, she hasn't bothered to hide this from her husband, because she knows he's in no position to leave her anyway.

Each evening, she comes home from work to have dinner with her children, cooked and served by her husband. When the children have disappeared to do their homework, she leaves to spend the night with her lover. Far from complaining about this arrangement or making ultimatums, her husband meekly accedes to the new routine without a word. In fact, since she's started the affair, he's so worried she'll divorce him that he's making a real effort, for the first time, to hold a conversation during dinner. She would leave him, but she can't afford to, since she would then have to support him and sell her house to give him half the equity. As things stand, his financial dependence allows her to arrange her life any way she likes, as long as she doesn't wish to remarry.

Her financial control has put her in the position more often experienced by husbands.

Another woman I know of presents an interesting case. A rich and celebrated agent for British and European television and movie stars, she's divorcing her husband of fifteen years, an artist who designs book and record jackets and who earns much less than she does. They can't agree on a settlement. She's seen several legal counselors who all want to take her case because its novelty will attract attention.

Joan Gordon (which is not her real name) is unarguably the most feared and powerful theatrical agent in London. She has commanded fees and payments for her clients that break all previous European records. The entertainment world is in awe of her. She is so effective at gaining the best terms for her client in any negotiation that one wonders why a producer would even want to deal with her. Her clients share in her aura—for it's clear that she has no time to represent anyone but actors who can demand a lot of money. She has perfected the art of getting the highest offer for her clients. As she confided to a friend, when she's negotiating a deal and the other person makes an offer, she remains utterly silent. Her silence is intimidating, communicating that the offer isn't even worthy of a reply. Invariably, the other person raises the offer, before she's said a single word.

She talks of her current divorce and sums it up this way: "I'm leaving my husband and I make more money—so I'm in the position of the man." She is now forty-two and earning a quarter of a million pounds a year. Her husband is sixty, and earning perhaps thirty-five thousand, which doesn't go very far when you live in London and have become accustomed to a life of luxury.

She has offered to pay him the proceeds from selling their weekend country house (about 200,000 pounds) and to pay for their sons' education. She's also offered him ten thousand pounds a year for the next five or six years. She feels that's all she owes—after all, he earns a decent wage, and she didn't deprive him of a career—he was a forty-five-year-old magazine designer when she met him.

He wants more and is in a panic about being left alone. He argues that he would have structured his career differently if it hadn't been for their marriage—that she had led him to believe she would always be there to support him if he devoted himself to creative work. He whines to her that she never asks him how he is, and he complains to the children that she doesn't give him any money, trying to shame her into being more generous.

Although previously she tried to dignify her marriage by thinking of him as creative and brilliant, now she makes no effort to conceal her contempt. "He's extremely dependent on me—not just financially. He's not a very competent person, you see."

While Gordon claims that she married her husband because she admired his intellect, some who know them don't believe that Gordon ever looked up to him. One of her friends insists that Gordon married her husband because he was a presentable social partner who accepted, even wanted, a dominating woman. Also, his work caused him to spend a lot of time alone and travel a great deal, so he wouldn't make too many demands on her.

Gordon admits that when she married him, she knew he loved her more than she loved him. She also knew she would never get hurt in this marriage. But now she thinks it's inappropriate for a successful businesswoman like herself to be married to a man who earns so little. However, she seems unaware that she's repeating her pattern.

For the last few months she's been dating a writer who is attempting to break into more commercial projects. In the meantime, he's living in a small flat she would never want to spend any time in. When they visit together, they stay in a suite that she pays for. She insists that he's totally different from her husband, competent and not at all dependent. Yet one wonders whether Gordon would be comfortable if she couldn't be sure she was in control.

While Gordon's situation reminds us that money stands behind much of what we assume to be masculinity, the fact remains that men are generally paid much more than women, and most men dominate their wives financially. Still, our cultural images reinforce stereotypes of women as frivolous spenders who make their exhausted husbands pay the bills.

Television stereotypes of feminine shopping compulsions, such as appear on *I Love Lucy*, have given way to images of single mothers who struggle to stretch every dollar and career women who haven't got a moment to shop because they're too busy preparing for another brilliant day in court. In fact, the department stores and shopping malls are still filled almost exclusively with women. For many women, shopping is a pleasant way to spend time with a friend, or have a little outing. Shopping as a form of relaxation or recreation is something most men still can't understand. When their wives go shopping, they view it as some form of female voodoo or revenge. A man I know insists that his ex-wife shopped and bought things she didn't need as a form of passive aggression. He's convinced that her shopping was a way of accusing him of being an inadequate provider and a failure as a man. In his view, she shopped to spend as much as she thought he should be earning and wasn't.

A therapist I talked to is convinced that in some marriages, shopping constitutes the main form of sex. Often the husband is impotent, and has withdrawn into compulsive work. The wife shops to calm herself and her frustrated anger, and though the husband pretends to object to her splurges, he secretly enjoys them. When she spends his money, for all the world to see, she is also displaying that her husband is a potent man.

Perhaps there is something libidinal, if not sexual, about shopping. Women who are always in search of the perfect purchase seem something like a female Don Juan—always looking, looking, looking, but never satisfied. Though many women use shopping to cheer themselves up, some of my friends say that when they're really depressed they can't find anything they want to buy. They drag themselves from store to store in the hope that something might arouse their interest, but nothing excites them. On the other hand, women who have had a successful day of shopping often come home wearing a look of satisfied exhaustion.

I think most women like to shop because it's a way to nurture themselves, and for some people this becomes a habitual way to feel better. I've also seen both men and women get most impulsive about spending when they're overwhelmed by unsatisfied needs. One psychoanalyst sees compulsive shopping as both an infantile pleasure and an act of provocation or revenge against ungiving parents. According to William Kaufmann, some people get momentary sensual pleasure from the power of spending money. More often, compulsive spenders are unconsciously seeking to force another person to take care of them by becoming financially dependent on the other:

Many such compulsive spenders maintain a reliable economic relationship with a member of the family or a friend who comes to his financial rescue whenever this help is needed. . . . Other compulsive spenders had neither money nor love in childhood. Their selfish spending in adulthood is an unconsciously overdetermined means of giving themselves something akin to love and at the same time creating debts which their relatives have to repay.[2]

One compulsive shopper I spoke with embodies this syndrome. Beverly Sharpe is a thirty-five-year-old wife and mother who lives in a luxurious apartment building in San Francisco with dramatic views of the bay. She received me in her carefully decorated living room, wearing expensive leather slacks and an angora sweater.

She had volunteered to tell me about her life because she believes she has a problem with money. She attributes its origin to the fact that her parents divorced when she was nine months old, and within two years her father was totally absorbed in his new family. She recalls how much it hurt when he told her he couldn't afford to buy her a bike or send her to camp, though she could see that he was clearly providing these things for his new little girl.

Beverly's mother came from an affluent family, so Beverly was showered with gifts from her mother and her uncles to compensate her for not having a father. As a child, she always had three coats for every season—one for play, one for school, one for dressy occasions—and she was always voted the best-dressed girl in the school. Every Saturday, her two bachelor uncles would take her to the toy store where she was allowed to choose whatever she wanted while they waited by the door.

By her own admission, Beverly was "looking to be comfortable" when she married, and the husband she chose filled the bill. He's an advertising executive who earns over $200,000 a year. But, Beverly complains, he's never home because he works so hard, and her children don't have enough of a father. She feels they're not really a family.

From the moment she said that I was sure that Beverly was reliving in her marriage the great disappointment of her childhood—her father's withdrawal, which could never be adequately compensated for by clothes and presents. Why do people repeat their early traumas? Some just automatically veer toward repetition, finding security in what is familiar. When people are compulsively driven to repeat painful scenarios over and over again, it's often a doomed effort to triumph over a traumatic experience by trying to make it end with a more desirable outcome.

In Beverly's case, there was even a projection of her childhood disappointment to the next generation. On behalf of her children, she is still protesting about not having a "real" family. Her need to overcome the pain of abandonment probably also lay behind her decisions about having children. A few years after they married, Beverly insisted on adopting two "hard to place" twins who were six years old at the time. Her husband was not enthusiastic about the idea, but he finally let her have her way. Feeling sorry for the children because they'd had such a hard time as orphans, she has always showered them with gifts. At Christmas alone, they each get twenty presents from their parents.

Beverly is also a compulsive spender on herself and her home. Her closets are stuffed with clothes she has no need for, and she has bought so many knick-knacks, placemats, candlesticks, and bowls that she had to put them in storage because there's no room for them in her apartment. This year, Beverly's husband bought her a new sports car to make up for the evenings he spends at work. But she tells me that she couldn't stop there. She had to go shopping for several pairs of leather pants and sweaters to go with the car, and then she just kept going and going.

She tells me her husband desperately needs two suits for work but he doesn't have the time to shop for them. She, on the other hand, has plenty of time to shop when the children are at school. She has considered getting a job but says the children still demand a lot of attention. Also, since most of her women friends have high-paying jobs (having worked ten years to get them) she can't imagine starting with an entry-level salary.

At one point, she ran up such huge bills on her credit cards that her husband took them all away. When they moved to San Francisco a few months ago, he opened a new checking account in his name alone, so she can't even cash checks at the supermarket. Every time she goes to the market, she has to bring along a note from her husband that gives her permission to cash his check. He gives her a "daily allowance," leaving $40 on the kitchen table every morning as he rushes off to work. He knows if he gives her more, she'll spend it.

Beverly is humiliated by this arrangement. She feels like a child being given lunch money. But this is precisely her unconscious goal—to use her spending habits to place herself in a dependent state and force her husband (father) to pay attention to her. She is charming and likable, and always manages to get more money, which, rebelliously, she spends. But the result is never satisfying because it's still not an adequate substitute for love lost. She's still not getting enough love.

To me, people who spend their own money freely, even impulsively, are appealing. It's those who spend other people's money who seem to have the problem—as well as those who always wind up paying for them. I've known only a few people who stayed in a marriage with a compulsive spender; in every case, they believed they had to pay for love.

One who comes to mind is a very bright and hardworking television producer I met several years ago. At the time she was thirty-two and had just gotten out of a short, disastrous marriage. Because she lacked self-confidence when it came to men, she had overlooked a lot of serious flaws in her husband. The one thing she couldn't overlook was his spending habits.

Amanda Morris grew up in a conservative, traditional, church-going family in southern California. Her grandparents, who lived two blocks away when she was a child, owned an egg ranch and a farm with citrus trees. The Morrises were simple people who paid for everything with cash—even automobiles. Nothing in her family was bought on payments or with loans, not even real estate.

Neither of her parents had gone to college. They both worked in a hardware store that formerly was a feedstore owned by Amanda's grandparents, and they were financially comfortable. Amanda was always achievement-oriented and responsible. She was the valedictorian of her class in a small-town high school. She was also a cheerleader, and is still an exceptionally pretty woman, although she has never regarded herself as successful with men. Because she was the high school "brain" in physics and math, she wasn't popular with boys, and one of her worst memories is being unable to find a date for a high school event in which she was specially honored.

Another early disappointment was her parent's refusal to send her to an Eastern college. Amanda had always dreamed of going to Smith, but her parents, unimpressed by the fact that she was an outstanding student, insisted that she go to a local junior college instead of spending all that money on a college in the East. With her record, she probably could have won a scholarship, but she couldn't apply for one because her parents refused to fill out the financial disclosure forms on the grounds that a person's income is no one else's business.

Amanda supported herself all the way through college, and after graduation she dabbled in Republican politics, the politics in which she was raised. While doing volunteer work in a senatorial election campaign, she became involved with a young man who worked as a professional campaign advisor. He was only the second man she had ever dated in a serious way, and though she didn't think that she really loved Ken, she let him talk her into marriage. From the first day, it was a disappointment. After badgering her to marry him for months, he arrived late to the wedding ceremony and told her on their wedding night that the marriage had probably been a mistake.

Two months after the wedding, she, herself, knew it was a mistake. Lacking experience and self-confidence, however, she kept telling herself that she wasn't making enough allowances for her husband. By this time, she was working as a production assistant for a television studio, and he was in business with two other partners as a political lobbyist. While she worked ten hours a day, Ken put in six hours at the office and complained when she didn't have dinner on the table. He also complained because she wouldn't change her name for his. Amanda's doubts about her marriage were piling up, but it was only her husband's spending patterns that forced her to see that he was seriously disturbed.

Just before we married [in 1980] he led me to believe he had fifteen thousand dollars he needed to invest, or he'd lose it in taxes, and he wanted to buy a house. My instincts were all telling me, no, don't get conned, but my father said that real estate was a good investment and he helped us get financing. So we bought a house for a hundred and thirty-four thousand dollars.

Once we started dealing with loan documents and credit reports I began to see how much money he owed. At the time, I was earning two hundred and fifty or three hundred dollars a week, but I always lived within my means. He told me he'd earned forty thousand dollars the previous year as a campaign manager. While we were filling out the forms I found out that he had two MasterCard accounts and two Visa accounts from different banks. He owed twenty-nine hundred dollars on one MasterCard account, and four thousand dollars to Carte Blanche. I thought to myself, God, this sounds like a lot. But he said it was nothing—he needed the interest charges for a tax write-off. I later learned you need to earn money before you can write off deductions. When we got home I asked him to tell me how much he owed. He did not give me an honest figure—he told me nine or ten thousand dollars. As it turned out, he owed thirteen thousand dollars on his credit cards. I told him I couldn't deal with it, so he cut up a couple of them, but he told me he had to keep the rest because he was an important person and had to look good on his job.

From the start, Amanda worried about the debts. A lot of them were from trips Ken had taken in Europe before they married. After they married, Ken continued to live high. Amanda thought they would just have to be careful and pay off the debts. Each month when they sat down to pay the bills she wanted to pay off some of the principal, but he wanted to pay only the minimum amount of interest. They also had big house payments. These had started at $1,200 dollars but soon went up to $1,400 dollars a month. Amanda told her husband they would have been better off using the $15,000 to pay off the debts instead of buying a house. He told her that she didn't understand anything about money. She tried not to nag, but with frightening bills coming in from the department stores, she always had to ask him whether he'd bought anything.

Amanda also liked to eat dinner out often, because she came home from work very late, but she wanted to have inexpensive meals—$10 for the two of them. Ken, however, always ordered the most expensive items on the menu and would take their friends to fancy restaurants. "He was very pretentious and liked to banter with the wine steward. Once he spent $800 on a dinner for eight people. He could remember a meal he ate in 1976. Food was like sex on a plate for him."

She knew that image was very important in politics and she put a lot of effort into his career, spending many awful hours sitting next to sexist politicians on the rubber chicken circuit. Three months after they were married, Ken was fired by his partners, who told him they would buy out his share of the business. Ken told Amanda it was nothing—people always get fired in nonelection years. But she was alarmed, knowing that he had no employment background. He applied for several jobs and didn't get any of them, partly because he always asked for too much money.

They were just able to make their payments, but Amanda was very tense. Ken had bladder problems that he ignored until she made him see a doctor, and then he had to go on muscle relaxants. She also discovered he had a terrible temper; he was always ranting and raving. She felt as though she had to walk on eggshells.

During this period Amanda got a great job offer to produce a television show in Washington, D.C., and she thought this would be perfect: a Republican administration was in control, and Ken would be able to find a job there. But Ken objected, blaming Amanda for the loss of his job and accusing her of trying to ruin his career. He finally agreed to the move because it would enable him to tell people that he had sacrificed his job for his wife, instead of admitting that he was fired.

Before they left California, they had to get their taxes in order, so they met with Ken's accountant. Now Amanda learned that Ken, who had earned $40,000 the previous year, had paid no withholding taxes and owed another $12,000. She broke down in tears.

When the time came to move, she was holding down two jobs—finishing a show in California and starting one in Washington. They agreed that all that Ken had to do was go to Washington in advance of the move and find a place for them to live. Instead, he ran into an old roommate from prep school and took off on a two-week jaunt. Amanda had to do all the packing while working at two jobs. He was still on his trip with his buddy when the moving truck came to pick up their furniture. The night before she got on the plane for Washington he called to say that he still hadn't found a place for them to live.

Naturally, when he did find a place it was bigger than they needed and more expensive than they could afford. It had six bedrooms and cost $1,300 a month (in current dollars, well over $2,000). She thought they should live in a smaller place, but Ken insisted he needed the house for his image and for big parties; anyway, he could write it off. The house was nice, but all Amanda could think about was how expensive it was.

By this time, she was feeling ill under the constant, tremendous stress. In addition, Ken was jealous of Amanda's time with him. If she worked late she got frantic phone calls from him, demanding to know why she wasn't home. When she wasn't in the same room with him at home, he'd call for her:

> I'd come home and there would be this big, weak thing, saying "Give Me, Give Me, Give Me, Hold Me, Fuck Me." As for our sex life, I couldn't stand it. In the best of times, it had been merely adequate. But sex was so important to him. It was the way he relaxed. It was always feed me, fuck me, take care of me. He wanted to feed off me, and I got nothing back.

Ken had bought two $600 suits so he'd look good, but Amanda recalls he was so overweight that the suits didn't help. "He's short and dumpy—he wears a size forty-two suit. I would try cooking vegetables for him, but his idea of a diet was to eat a whole cauliflower smeared with butter and parmesan cheese. To this day, I can't look at cauliflower."

The house they rented in Washington had a basement with a washer and dryer. One night Amanda was down there and didn't hear Ken calling for her because the dryer was going. Then she heard him bellowing her name, and she ran upstairs to see what was wrong. Frustrated because she hadn't appeared immediately, he picked up a spatula and hit her with it.

At that moment, Amanda knew she had to get out of the marriage. She needed time to find a place to live, but first she wanted to go back to California to find out whether she'd be responsible for his debts. For two months, she plotted her escape—"Every time I spread my legs I told myself I had to find a place to live." By August, Ken found a job as a lobbyist that paid $40,000 a year, so she told him she wanted to go to California on her own for a vacation. "He wanted to take off from his job and go with me, but I told him, no, you can't take off from a job you just started. He fought with me all the way to the airport and on the check-in line at the terminal. I turned around to the people behind us and said, 'Would you like to be married to this man?' "

When Amanda got back from California she found an apartment for $300 a month and got ready for the move. Finding an apartment had taken three weeks because she knew no one in Washington; she still didn't have a single friend there. Before telling him she was leaving, she removed all the things that mattered to her because she feared he might destroy everything in the house. While he was at work, she moved her cats because she was afraid he would take a butcher knife and stab them when he discovered she was leaving. She broke the news to him just before he had to leave on a business trip so he'd be away when he was most enraged. The night he found out she was leaving she had to produce a television show, and she checked into a hotel so he couldn't find her.

In the end, Amanda lost all her savings to end the marriage. When she met Ken later to work out a separation agreement, he offered to buy her out of the house they owned together for $2,000. In fact, Amanda had contributed thousands of dollars in mortgage payments, and she had sold her car to pay off some of his debts. When she asked him what she was supposed to get out of all the payments she'd made on the house, he told her that she'd had the privilege of living there. She told him he was crazy, and stormed out, but later, her lawyer convinced her that going to court would be too expensive. Unable to take any more strain, she gave him her share of the house for $2,000.

For me, Amanda's story illustrates how even the most self-deluding person is forced to face the truth when confronted with monetary evidence. Raised to be a good and uncomplaining girl, and to suppress her feelings in the service of others, Amanda took a great deal of abuse. Interestingly, it was money that finally released her from the habit of female accommodation. Had she been financially dependent on her husband, she might have talked herself into understanding him for another twenty years, as many women do who are beaten or abused. While she was able to rationalize his infantile behavior in other areas of life, it was those cold, hard figures on the credit card statements that allowed her to see how infantile and disturbed he truly was.

It would be nice to think that in marriage and nonmarital relationships, people could maintain an adult attitude even when circumstances force one to be financially supported by the other. Unfortunately, in today's world, this is nearly impossible, even when the dependent partner is making an equal contribution by doing the child care and housekeeping. Being financially dependent is a set-up for becoming a child. In these times, anyone who would choose this position for an extended period is probably looking for a parent-substitute. Those who keep forcing others to pay for their expenses are symbolically extracting revenge from a parent who, they believe, neglected them.

What's the solution? All adults need to be self-supporting or, at least, know they *could* earn enough to meet all their needs. Until we have decent and affordable child-care, the necessity of being self-supporting is most problematic for those with young children. But the undermining forces of being financially dependent takes its emotional toll on middle-class spouses and partners just as it does on adults who live off their parents or those who are financially dependent on welfare and the state. Children and those who are sick and old obviously need to be supported. All others need to be able to support themselves.

8

•

Parents and Children

A common theme in stories about money is the role it plays either in binding people to their parents or in providing them with a means to break away. The connection between money and parents can be literal—as when financial dependence forces children to live with their parents or do what they want—or it can be more symbolic—as when upwardly mobile people discover a world outside the confines of what their parents could have imagined and see money as the means of attaining that world.

Most of us are ambivalent about our attachment to parents. The wish to separate from our parents is typically joined with an opposing tendency to remain attached—either by dependence, or by reliving the conflicts or plots of their lives and through this largely unconscious identification keeping them with us.

In our culture of self-made identity, where each person bears personal responsibility for achieving fulfillment, many of us have a theory about the tragic flaws in our parents' lives—the weaknesses or mistakes that blocked them from achieving happiness. Some believe their parents' downfall was their marriage, while others believe a parent's life was ruined because of failure to pursue the occupation that was his or her passion.

People who are psychologically oriented often pin the blame on a personal trait or inhibition that kept their parents from acting in their own interest, and they worry lest the same inclination infect their own lives. Usually, the reappearance of the failing in their own lives takes them by surprise. A man I know wryly observes that although he did everything possible to enter into a marriage that would bear no resemblance to the relationship of his parents,

95

he realized upon divorce that he had married his mother and become his father.

Other people tend to see money as a strong mediating factor in their parents' defeat, and they rely on money to provide an escape route from a similar fate. Like the man who gets out of bed and counts his money when he's feeling anxious and unable to sleep, they use money to ward off the terrors of childhood.

One way or another, most of us look to money to free us. In many ways, this makes sense. Our fates are sealed by a few factors: luck, talent, psychological inclination, and opportunity—and money is often the main ingredient in the circumstances that create or remove opportunity. But when it comes to intimate relationships, to the ways we experience love and attachment with partners and children, money cannot really free us from the formative patterns that seem to gel early in life.

It was Sigmund Freud who first clearly laid out the idea that love is an illusion, and that we are blind to the realities of our loved ones and project onto them and the current situation the lingering traumas of the past. Freud believed that all adult love is built on the scaffolding of transference: our tendency to repeat, over and over, something forgotten that happened early in life. As Janet Malcolm observed in her brilliant essay on psychoanalysis, the idea that we are practically doomed to repeat the past is perhaps the most fundamental and disturbing principle in the psychoanalytic canon:

> The phenomenon of transference—how we all invent each other according to early blueprints—was Freud's most original and radical discovery. The idea of infant sexuality and of the Oedipus complex can be accepted with a good deal more equanimity than the idea that the most precious and inviolate of entities—personal relations—is actually a messy jangle of misapprehensions, at best an uneasy truce between solitary fantasy systems. Even (or especially) romantic love is fundamentally solitary, and has at its core a profound impersonality. The concept of transference at once destroys faith in personal relations and explains why they are tragic: we cannot know each other. We must grope around for each other through a dense thicket of absent others. We cannot see

each other plain. A horrible kind of predestination hovers over each new attachment we form.[1]

Although it is currently fashionable to try tossing much of Freudian dogma into the trashbin of history, in fact, most of his ideas have filtered down inextricably into the major psychological doctrines of the moment. Most clinicians, of whatever persuasion, take as a given the tendency for people to repeat and relive ungratifying experiences in the often vain attempt to master them. Not only is repetition assumed to play a major role in any individual life, but current dogma advances the view that conflicts and patterns of behavior are often passed from generation to generation. Even in contemporary popular culture there's a widespread notion that children who were abused abuse their own children, that survivors of incest, or alcoholic parents, and so forth, have incorporated their parents' pathology into their own way of life.

There are different explanations for the route of transmission. Many psychologists accept the idea of parental identification: that we unconsciously model our lives on the lives of our parents. More recently, some psychologists talk about "mirroring," the process by which children oblige their parents by becoming reflections of their parents' projections. Either way, there is a reproduction of conflicts and unsatisfied needs from generation to generation.

One way or another, unconscious repetition is a major element in life, whether it be repeating a formative trauma in the hope of mastering it or repeating a scenario passed from generation to generation. Of course we struggle to escape these destinies at the same time that we unerringly pursue them. Into these plots, money is embroidered as a major subplot, representing, as it often does, an illusion of freedom. A talented and successful writer I know provides a curious example.

Susan Bryce is a forty-six-year-old filmmaker from Los Angeles. She is highly respected in the film world and by those who work in public television for her original and acclaimed documentaries about contemporary American life. Her parents climbed from dirt poor to rich but, according to Susan, they never found a home in their long march upward. Susan is the oldest child, and all her younger siblings have reverted to the life-style of their parents' Irish, working-class youth. Susan was the talented child who carried the contradictions of her family's mobility into the next generation.

When she was born in 1944, her eighteen-year-old father worked in a food-processing factory in the South, and her seventeen-year-old mother cleaned rooms in a boarding house. Susan grew up with stories of her parents' extreme poverty during the depression: living in tents, going hungry, owning only the clothes on their backs when they married. Her father's brothers, also unskilled workers, made a life out of drinking, fighting, and brawling. But Susan's father was remarkably talented. He rose quickly in the ranks of the workers and won a scholarship to get college training in agriculture during the late 1940s. Eventually he rose to the top ranks of management in the emerging processed foods industry.

As her father ascended in the business, the family moved all over the country, never living anywhere for more than a year or two and always renting rather than buying. As they got richer, the home furnishings changed, and Susan's mother acquired matched bedroom and living room sets, always in atrocious taste according to Susan, because they were moving into a class her mother knew nothing about.

Dimly grasping what culture she should be bringing to her family, Susan's mother tried to introduce books and reading into the household, but she could never get her husband to read or take an interest in other middle-class refinements. Though he was now surrounded at work by people who had liberal arts educations, Susan's father had enormous contempt for all highbrow culture and would come home from work, get drunk, and fall asleep.

Susan was always the smart child destined to go far, her father's favorite and the flagbearer for her mother's middle-class aspirations. By the time Susan went to Radcliffe College in 1962, her father was earning $50,000 a year. Not wanting her to become soft, however, he created artificial deprivation for her by providing no money beyond what she had to pay for room and board.

Even today, Susan's father is a mass of contradictions. Though he earns a huge salary, he has never saved or invested his money, and he's given almost nothing to his children, even when they've badly needed it. Instead, he spends the money on expensive clothes, big cars, a fancy house. When he takes Susan out for lunch in expensive restaurants with menus he can't understand, he passes out large bills to the wine steward to make sure he'll be fawned over, or ten dollars to the hat-check girl so she'll flirt with him. Yet like many who have achieved mobility, he feels contempt for the class he approached but never joined. In Susan's opinion, his happiest days were the early ones spent in the factory with his buddies, and his life was ruined by leaving the working class.

In the years before Susan left for college her parents suffered enormously from the constant moves and loss of ties. They fought constantly, and after their marriage fell apart her mother drank heavily and twice tried to kill herself. Miraculously, her mother eventually found the cultured life she'd always wanted: she married a college professor and got a college degree herself. But after all that, she still could get only the low-level jobs that were available to her before, and when she was fifty-two she died of a combination of alcohol and sleeping pills. Susan is convinced that money destroyed both her parents: "There was a whole tragic theme—they had come from nothing, and through hard work my father made a lot of money and it was shit. The money didn't help—my father was drinking because he felt sick at what he became. In my mind, the family deteriorated socially as we advanced economically."

Although Susan escaped the self-destructive patterns of her parents' lives, she relives the contradictions of their class identifications. Soon after finishing college she fulfilled her mother's ambition by choosing a husband who fit her mother's ideal: a Jewish art professor who had been educated at Harvard and knew all about good wines, classical music, gourmet cooking, and oriental rugs. The marriage was not satisfying to Susan—they were more like work colleagues than lovers—and eventually she left her intellectual husband to live with a blue-collar factory worker who is dedicated to union organizing. Having first fulfilled her mother's dream (while identifying with her father and ridiculing her husband's taste as pretentious) she left the Harvard graduate for an uneducated man who fits her romantic image of her father as a rebellious young man and honest laborer, the man she imagines her father was before he was destroyed by middle-class success and her mother's aspirations. Now she's surprised at herself when she acts as her mother did, trying to teach her unpolished companion some of the niceties of middle-class life. Her comparison of sitting down to dinner with each of her partners is revealing:

Andy [Susan's first husband] would cook the dinners—I was responsible for the cleaning—and we'd have a long meal and talk about books and ideas. Our friends all had graduate educations and were middle-class intellectuals. Our social life was very structured—dinner parties that Andy planned because he was the better cook.

Paul eats just to get the food inside him, and he's finished with dinner in ten minutes. The other day he started to clear his plate while I was still eating, and I screamed at him never to do that again. The only foods he likes are beef, potatoes, and spaghetti. He won't eat fish. If he cooked, he would always make chopped meat and macaroni with onions and tomato sauce. Andy is a wine connoisseur and Paul doesn't know a thing about wine. My son always comes home from visits with his father with his taste upgraded—suddenly he's asking for spaghetti carbonara and steak au poivre.

Andy can talk your ear off, and he speaks in whole paragraphs. His Harvard education wasn't wasted. When he came home he would announce some topic sentence and theme: "Something happened to me today that illustrates the blah, blah, blah." But Paul has trouble just getting the words out of his mouth. When something happens to him at work, he'll come home and we'll have ten minutes of "god damn . . . I can't . . . they just . . ." I have to ask him what, when, and where, like a journalist. It takes him ten minutes just to get his thoughts into sentences and a long time to organize his ideas. He's very inhibited about leaping into words. My life with Paul is much more ad hoc—nothing is planned. I don't know how much money there will be in six months, and Paul's comfortable with that. Whereas Andy would always have things planned out and systematized so there would be no shocks or surprises."

Once they divorced, Susan's first husband drifted to a more "yuppie" life-style, moving into a fancy Los Angeles condominium while Susan moved into a ramshackle house in a working-class neighborhood. Never that comfortable or impressed with middle-class values, there are things she doesn't like about Andy's influence on the children: "After the kids were with him they came back with the idea that they should go to a fancy summer camp. I don't see why they should, but maybe I'm creating artificial deprivation the way my father did." Her children have two men as models in their lives, just as Susan knew two men in her father, the factory worker and the executive: "One day my son will say he'll be a truckdriver and do a macho imitation of Paul . . . but he's not a tough kid, he's a reader. He and my daughter must notice the difference when they go from one place to another."

Divided by a desire to rescue her father and restore the integrity he once had, before he made a fortune and lost his early ties, and her mother's wish for an educated and civilized life, Susan lives between two worlds. Ironically, she can't stop herself from trying to teach her new partner better table manners, as her mother once did with her father. Socially, her life is as polarized as her family background and her choice of men. At home, she is surrounded by working class neighbors and Paul's friends from work. In her work, Susan mixes with an intellectual and artistic elite. Every day of her life is a reminder of how people are displaced by the acquisition or loss of money, and despite enormous intelligence and insight, Susan is still caught up in the conflicts of her parents' marriage.

I know other women who have unconsciously reenacted a childhood wish to rescue their fathers in their choice of husbands. One woman I know, Katherine Elliot, even recognized the connection, but it didn't deter her.

Katherine was born into an old and distinguished New England family. Among her ancestors are civic leaders and philanthropists who are legendary in American history; in and around Boston, towns and the streets bear their names. While Katherine's extended family generally held to the principle of conserving inheritances so that future generations would be protected and provided for, Katherine's own father was the profligate black sheep. Both her mother and father were serious alcoholics, and they never considered their own futures or those of their children. Instead of investing their money, they squandered it on extravagant trips and lavish parties. Instead of establishing trust funds for his children, Katherine's father spent his inheritance on himself. Although Katherine was a highly intelligent and serious student, her father objected to sending her to college and urged her to marry well instead.

Her mother died when Katherine was twenty, and her father died soon after. Although Katherine's two younger brothers were only twelve and sixteen, their father left no provision for them—no life insurance policy and only minor savings. When Katherine was forced to take over the upbringing of her brothers, she discovered that her father hadn't even paid income taxes for the past fifteen years, and when he died, he owed $40,000 in medical bills.

Because she had to assume responsibility for her brothers when she might have been focusing on her own education and career, Katherine was temporarily sidetracked, but eventually her talent and hard work led to impressive professional credentials and an interesting career in law. Her strong identification with being upper-class always steered her toward people who came from privileged backgrounds. She could spot them by name or by manner wherever she went, and she was always drawn to those social worlds—philanthropic foundations, voluntary organizations, and boards of trustees—where people with old money were likely to collect. Deprived of her inheritance, she managed through hard work and ambition to regain her place in the world she'd been born to.

More than a few men fell in love with Katherine and wanted to marry her, but she could never commit herself to any of the doctors, lawyers, and businessmen who had achieved success through their own efforts. Instead, when she married, she chose a man who reminded her of her father: charming, spoiled, and irresponsible: "He has inheritances and pending inheritances, and a sense of entitlement. I have a sense of responsibility for doing things for one's family but Randall is more like my father. He spends his money on himself and he doesn't want to work." She smiled as she recounted his weaknesses. "He hasn't got a shred of ambition. He'd rather not work because he likes sports, and if he had a regular job, how could he take off for four days at a time, to go skiing? He's a happy person. He likes the outdoors and he'd be glad to live off my earnings and his trust fund." Randall also brought to their marriage a son from his previous marriage. Once again, Katherine was responsible for raising a boy who was not her own child, just as she had taken over the care of her father's sons.

Katherine knew she was taking a big risk when she married Randall, for in addition to his lack of ambition he had a bad marital record; he had been divorced twice before. But the fact that she had known and loved him when she was very young (there was an earlier involvement between them twelve years before) and the fact that he was so much like her father must have convinced her that this marriage was her romantic destiny.

Predictably, it was a disaster, and after a few years Katherine tired of taking care of a man who refused to grow up. When she married again she broke from her usual pattern and chose her first husband's apparent social antithesis—not a pleasure-seeking child living off trust funds but a distinguished businessman who has earned success through talent and hard work.

The repetition of early love experiences is carried not only into marriages but also into the next generation. Here, too, money plays a revealing role in reproducing formative scenarios. The history of one woman I came to know illustrates how a huge windfall of money can't change the emotional course of a lifetime. It's the story of Teresa Cuneo, who lived by the conviction that mothers and daughters can't coexist.

Perhaps every girl is occasionally struck with the disturbing idea that her own existence has been carved out of the flesh of her mother's. In dark moments, who hasn't recognized that one life is often saved or nurtured at the expense of another? According to Teresa Cuneo, on the day her life began, her mother's life was ruined.

Her mother had been raised a devout Catholic in a small town in Yugoslavia. Only weeks before she was to marry, Teresa's mother discovered she was pregnant. When she told her fiance, he denied being the father of the child and broke off the relationship. Because of the shame of her condition (in 1921), she went off alone to Romania to have the child. Two-and-a-half-years later, her mother brought Teresa back to Yugoslavia and left the little girl to be raised by her grandmother. Teresa's mother escaped her stigmatized life by moving to the United States.

Teresa saw her mother only once during the next ten years, but when she was twelve, her mother suddenly returned and took her to New York. Teresa was miserable and for months she cried to be allowed to return to her "mother." I *am* your mother," she was scolded, and eventually Teresa gave in and accepted the situation.

At first, Teresa was sent to a strict Catholic boarding school, but she did so poorly that at fifteen she dropped out and went to beauty school. Within a year, she was working in a beauty parlor and turning over most of her salary to her mother. About this time she also started to date a man who worked as a waiter in the restaurant next to her shop. The girl's emerging sexuality made her mother hysterical. When Teresa went out on dates, her mother would lock her out if she returned a few minutes after midnight and accuse her of being a tramp. Teresa's mother's life had been ruined by sex, and she was obsessed with its place in her daughter's life. Unable to bear living with her mother any longer, Teresa decided to marry the waiter.

In 1942 Teresa's husband was drafted and sent into combat and Teresa, at 21, gave birth to a daughter. Following her own mother's example, Teresa left the child in the care of its grandmother—in this case, her husband's mother who lived in Massachusetts, while Teresa continued to work in the beauty parlor. Her husband returned from the war shell-shocked, violent, and abusive.

Eventually, they divorced, but in the process Teresa lost custody of her daughter, Irene. The child had been living with Teresa's mother-in-law, and as Teresa tells the story, when the judge asked the six-year-old child whether she wanted to go with her mother, the girl answered that she needed to go home with her grandmother. Teresa was given visitation rights, but only under restrictive conditions.

A few years later, Teresa remarried, this time choosing a taxi driver whose wife had just been struck and killed by an automobile while she tried to cross Eastern Parkway in Brooklyn pushing a baby carriage. When Teresa told her mother she was marrying, her mother remarked that Frank Cuneo was marrying her only because he needed a woman to take care of his two young children. Teresa retorted that she would not wind up alone and miserable like her mother.

Teresa had problems with her stepchildren but got on well with her new husband. When they grew up, her stepson, Steven, became a policeman and her stepdaughter, Mary, worked as a salesclerk after dropping out of high school. At first, her stepdaughter was more of a problem than the boy. Having become pregnant, Mary married a man who treated her badly. From time to time, she would show up at her parents' apartment with a black eye and a suitcase. According to Teresa, she always needed money for something. When Mary's own son grew up and turned eighteen he left home, and to this day, no one in the family knows where he is. It's a family where parents and children always seem to be losing each other.

In 1963 Teresa developed an allergy to the chemicals used in cosmetic products, and she stopped working for a year. She doesn't know whether it was because of staying home or the effect of menopause, but she had what her doctors called a nervous breakdown and had to be hospitalized for a few months. When she came home, she realized that she needed to get out of the house, and in 1965 she took a part-time job doing janitorial work in a Manhattan office building. By the time Teresa retired in 1984 she was taking home $189 dollars a week. She paid for the groceries out of her earnings and kept the rest to spend on anything she liked—clothes, bingo, gifts for the grandchildren, trips to Atlantic City to play blackjack. Frank paid the rent on their Brooklyn apartment, and all the other expenses. They both liked to gamble—each year they saved $2,000 for a trip to Las Vegas.

In 1975 Teresa and Frank had a big fight with Frank's son, Steven. Frank and his son had owned a small boat as partners, but when Teresa became ill and needed an abdominal operation, Frank had to sell the boat to pay for the hospital bills. While Teresa was still in the hospital, Steven called and asked for $1,500, his share of the proceeds. Frank sent him a check but refused to talk with him after that, and Steven refused to apologize. For nine whole years they did not exchange a word. At first, Teresa would send cards and gifts to Steven's children on Christmas and birthdays, but eventually she stopped.

In 1984, while coming home from work at midnight, Teresa was mugged. Since the incident occurred in the precinct where Steven was a policeman she took this opportunity to call him for advice about how to recover her property. It was close to Christmas, and they exchanged greeting cards. Eventually, Teresa and Frank made a date to go to Steven's house for dinner on a Sunday in early spring. Not a word was said about the nine-year rift.

On the day Frank Cuneo was to see his son for the first time in nine years, he rose at seven and opened the Sunday newspaper to check the winning lottery numbers. The number given for the million-dollar prize was the one he'd been playing for the past month. His ticket stub was in a drawer in the bedroom, but he didn't look at it right away. First he poured himself a beer, then he retrieved the slip of paper. It was the number.

Still unconvinced that he'd won, he woke Teresa and showed her the newspaper and his receipt. "You do have the six numbers," she agreed, "but don't get your high hopes up—it could be a mistake."

Now he called a friend from work and read the numbers on his ticket to her, so she could compare them to the winning numbers printed in her copy of the newspaper. They matched. Since it was Sunday, Frank and Teresa didn't know whom to call or what to do. They called Irene, Teresa's daughter, and carried the news to their reunion with Frank's son.

Late that night, when the Cuneos returned to their Brooklyn apartment, they found a telegram under the door. It was from the public relations director of the lottery. It said, "Congratulations. Do you know you have won the lottery? We can't tell you exactly how much you have won until Tuesday but we would like to see you tomorrow. Please call me immediately."

Since there were no other winners, the prize money came to over $2 million. Frank had been planning to retire anyway, but he and Teresa quit their jobs that day and moved to a suburb of Baltimore, near Teresa's daughter.

Frank, always a happier person than his wife, took pleasure in the fortune. He'd expected to retire to a modest apartment in Maryland, but now he bought a four-bedroom house with an above-ground pool and a brand new Cadillac. He liked working around the house, and when that first winter came he was grateful that he no longer had to rise at five-thirty and spend the day driving around in freezing weather.

Teresa's story was different, because money couldn't alter the course of her unhappiness. Like the characters in the 1950s television series *The Millionaire*, money merely revealed the person she'd become, it could not change her. Only months after they were settled into their new house, Teresa was brooding about the jealousies that festered in her family and grieving for what she had lost.

Frank was to receive only $50,000 from the lottery during the first year. After that, he'd be getting $200,000 a year for a decade. Though Teresa now led a more comfortable life, she was miserable with her new dependence on her husband. As long as she worked as a janitor, she always had her own money to spend on what she pleased. Now she had to ask Frank for money every time she needed to go to the supermarket, since he was managing the checkbook. She was also unhappy about the way he'd chosen to spend the first $50,000. Rather than buy a house and a Cadillac, she would have been happier using the money for gambling excursions and little presents for her grandchildren. Teresa liked to go out, and her husband was happier staying at home. Since winning the lottery, they had gone out to dinner only a couple of times, because, as he put it, "I'd rather eat at home. We're not used to it." When Teresa complained, he begged her to be patient until the "big money" started rolling in the next year—then he would set up a $5,000 account for Teresa's spending money. But this only irked her more when she considered how little this was compared with the $200,000 he'd be getting:

> I know he can't do that much right now, but I think he can
> do better. If I say I want to play bingo he gives me twenty
> dollars or thirty dollars, or if I want to go to Atlantic City
> to play blackjack, I have to ask him, and sometimes he says
> no. I used to go to Atlantic City more when I worked my-
> self. I did not want him to buy the Cadillac or the house.
> We could have gone to Las Vegas or Europe if we didn't
> have all these crazy bills—not sit here with the house. I
> don't have my own money and I feel sad. I miss my friends
> and I want to go back to work. I don't like this life. I said
> to him I wish he didn't win the lottery.

The winnings stirred up even worse problems with the children. Each of them had been given about $2,000 out of the first year's portion, but they weren't satisfied:

> When we gave the fifteen hundred dollars to Mary [Frank's
> daughter] I said to her, go to the dentist, have your teeth
> fixed. She said, no, mother, I have to pay for my car. Now
> she came yesterday, and borrowed another sixteen hun-
> dred dollars from my husband, because she needed it for
> her teeth. I don't mind giving her the money—it's just that
> she asked for it at the wrong time. I wish she had gone to
> the dentist before, but she doesn't listen and she's forever

asking for help. She used to come home to us whenever her husband beat her up, and then we wouldn't see her for five months—and she lived only a few blocks away. I said to myself—what's this, they only come when they need help? I said to my husband yesterday, give her the money, but when I ask you for forty dollars, give it to me, too. I didn't even tell my daughter that my stepdaughter was here yesterday for her teeth, because Irene would pass a remark like "All of a sudden she's here for the money when she didn't visit you when you lived five blocks away from her in Brooklyn."

My daughter is very jealous, and she has no right to be, because she got more than anybody else. She got a trip to Las Vegas plus a thousand dollars, and if she helped us she has always been well paid for her efforts. Each time I came here to visit her I came loaded with stuff. When she found this house for us I gave her a hundred dollars to pay her for the running around she did. When we moved into this house she said to me, "Mom, don't worry, I've got plenty of workers to help you get it cleaned up." I said, "Irene, you know I'm fussy. I can do it one room at a time." But she insisted on sending eleven or twelve kids over here, my grandson Jeffrey and his friends, and you know how they work—forget it. I gave my grandson twenty-five dollars to get pizza and soda for the kids and they ate and they drank. In the afternoon, it was another thirty-five dollars for more pizza and drinks, and then my husband gave each of them ten dollars for helping out. Then, my daughter said to my husband, "Frank, I think the kids would like it if you took them out for dinner."

We figured we would go to dinner at Roy Rogers or Wendy's. My daughter—she picks out class, Turf and Surf—seventeen dollars apiece for eleven kids. My dinner was the cheapest—eight or nine dollars, the rest of them cost sixteen or seventeen. For two hundred dollars plus twenty-five dollars for pizza plus another thirty-five plus the ten dollars he gave each of them, I could have had a private maid here for three weeks to do the job. That's my daughter.

Then my daughter had the gall to tell me that her husband would come over and help us put up the drapes if we would pay him. She said, "You can't expect my husband to come over here and do chores without being reimbursed." I said, "Irene, I would never ask anyone to do anything without getting paid." That's why, to this day, I haven't asked her for help. If there's something we can't do, we hire someone. She told me she'd send over my grandson to help—I should give him a couple of dollars. I don't think that's very bright. If you're a mother, you say, I'll send my son over and don't you dare give him anything. I told my daughter to be patient—if we live to be ninety-nine we'll never spend all this money. I told her, the first year the money should be for us, we don't have that long to live. I told her, "Don't worry, you'll gain by it and your children will gain by it, and even your children's children will gain by it." I don't care how nice the kids are—they're all looking for a piece of the action.

Before we won the lottery, when my daughter put on a retirement party for my husband she wrote to my stepson and invited him. His wife wrote back and said, "I'm sorry, we can't come." After we won the lottery, they came. Now we'll never know if they would have made up with us if we hadn't won. Before we won, my daughter Irene used to try to get us to make up with Frank's son. Now that we've seen him a few times she says, "The table has turned and he'll come out smelling like a rose."

I think she has gall to say to my husband, you can't expect my husband to come here and help you without getting paid. When I was young my mother was so mean to me, but I went there every week to clean for her. I shopped, I painted, and I never wanted to take a cent from her. If she made me take money, because she was very proud, I'd use it to bring her little baby lamb chops or a steak or a freshly killed chicken. Never did I want to take anything from my mother, and this is what hurts me. It just kills me. They're just waiting for me to die and for my husband to die so they can get the money.

I said to my daughter, thank God, if anything happens to my husband I won't be a burden on you. I'd go in a home or I'd have a private nurse. I often think, without the lottery would all this be the same? Would you say you can't expect my husband to come here and put up the curtains without reimbursement? It's nice to have money, but it's not what it's cracked up to be.

Teresa Cuneo may well have wished not to be like her mother, but she can hardly help it. "I will not be alone and miserable like you," she had told her mother forty years before. But, today, surrounded by her family, Teresa grieves and feels used, deserted, and alone. Abandoned by her mother at birth, then separated from her grandmother, she was destined to lose her own daughter when the child chose to live with her grandmother. The family drama, established by her own unwanted and disastrous conception, was built around the conviction that mothers and daughters can't coexist. Sixty-five years later, Teresa's life is dominated by the pain of believing her daughter wishes her dead so she won't have to wait for the money.

Freud once remarked that money can't bring joy because having it's not an original, infantile desire. Money is also not that helpful in freeing us from the conflicts and vulnerabilities established early in life. Yet money can serve as a kind of litmus test revealing our deepest feelings, which might not otherwise become conscious. It's not money, but the revelation of repressed emotions that allow some people to change the patterns of their relationships. I would not count Teresa Cuneo among those who are likely to find greater happiness in their family life, but others, like Amanda Morris and Katherine Elliot, have a chance to learn from the lessons of cold cash about the dangers of the men who attract them, and to break out of the pattern. As one wise therapist has concluded, "We are defeated in work and in love, but keep going. Though now we know the defeat to be in the nature of things and so unavoidable, we keep trying, hoping still to achieve when all hope has gone an unexpected victory."[2]

9

— • —

What Price Justice?

*T*he conviction that money can compensate for pain or loss is not merely an illusion, the principle is built into the American legal system. In court, Americans seek financial compensation for lost limbs, lost youth, lost love. Even what we take to be the most sacred, priceless object—a child—turns out to have a dollar value after all according to our courts, which award money for parental suffering in the wrongful death of a child.

There is still some ambiguity in the legal status of compensating for emotional damage in marriage or the pain of loss when a partner wants a divorce. Today, the courts generally try to divide marital property according to straight numerical formulas rather than by considering fault or pain and suffering. This is the guiding principle of "no-fault" divorce. It often comes as a shock to divorcing wives who try to show a judge how badly they've been treated, only to discover that the judge isn't interested. But although marital "faults" and emotional damage are increasingly irrelevant to the law, they are still routinely introduced into the testimony and usually have an impact on the awards.

The odd relation between love and money is most brilliantly illuminated by looking at the claims that are brought every day to our courtrooms, for they reveal not only the legal perspective but the lay principles of justice that ordinary people invoke when they attempt to convert feeling into dollars. A good example is the case of *Keller v. Keller*, a divorce trial I observed in New York State Supreme Court several years ago, not long after the principle of "equitable distribution" had been introduced into state law. According to the new law, all property acquired during marriage (other than inheritances) is considered the property of both spouses and subject to some kind of division upon divorce, regardless of who earned it. But at the time of the *Keller* trial, no one knew *how* the courts would define equity and what share of the property would go to each spouse. Because each case was setting a precedent, the trials were long and detailed. I took this opportunity to watch several cases over a period of a year, and I've chosen to write about one that raises all the familiar problems of using money to achieve justice.

When I first saw them, the Kellers sat on opposite ends of a large oak table facing the judge. I didn't know this couple, but I had come to observe their divorce trial as a place where love and betrayal would be measured in dollars and cents.

It wasn't just money that brought the Kellers to this theater. Every divorce trial is a morality play and a place for purging emotions. The Kellers had made their lives on the stage—Simon as a former actor, Veronika Clare as a singer. Like figures in a Greek tragedy, Simon Keller and Veronika Clare didn't know what was in them or what would come out of them; they needed the catalysts of chorus and audience to find out.

Veronika Clare was in constant motion, riffling through piles of papers and documents spread across her end of the table. She was high-strung and tiny—only four feet ten and a half inches tall, as she would remind the court when it considered her shrinking prospects for making a stage comeback at age fifty-four. Her dyed red hair was cut short in pixie style, and she wore an oversized sweater, narrow skirt, and six-inch spiked heels. Viewed from behind, she looked like a child dressed in her mother's clothes, but when she turned around Veronika Clare's face looked shockingly dark and wasted.

Mr. Heinz, Veronika Clare's lawyer, was heavy, bloated, and calm. Though Heinz was in his fifties, he was a newcomer to the divorce courts. After spending most of his career doing corporate law, he had drifted a few years earlier to employment in a U.S. government office in the Caribbean, and had just returned to New York and low-paying work in the offices of Leonard Price, who is well known as one of New York's meanest divorce lawyers. Rich and famous divorce contestants get Price himself to defend them. Those who are less endowed wind up with a staff member like Heinz. Sluggish and disorganized, Heinz took naturally to one of the perennial strategies of wives' attorneys—using endless delays and interminable searches for hidden funds to exhaust the husband into a better settlement.

As I watched from behind, Veronika Clare kept jumping up from her seat to search through heaps of her husband's financial records and income tax returns. Even standing, she was barely taller than the attorney sitting beside her. As Veronika and Heinz foraged through the banks of his papers, Simon Keller watched from the other side of the table, following their movements with a frozen stare. Off the witness stand, he referred to them as Fatty and The Midget.

Si Keller and his lawyer, Mark Singer, both age forty, were noticeably younger than the other pair. Dressed in similar outfits—well-cut suits, custom-made shirts, and Rolex watches—they might have been business associates or friends. Simon's curly grey hair had receded prematurely into a horseshoe. Combined with his angry demeanor, this made him look a bit like an old-fashioned gangster, hypertensive and aggressive. Mark Singer was smaller and handsome in the style of Upper East Side bachelors. Always straightening his clothes and tucking in his monogrammed shirt, he was constantly aware of his appearance. Just barely into July, Singer had a deep tan from weekends in the Hamptons, and under his dark jacket sleeve was the hint of a thin gold bracelet. According to Veronika, Simon and his lawyer looked like a pair of Las Vegas gamblers.

A few years ago, this would have been a different trial. It might have revolved around adultery—for Simon had affairs almost from the start of the marriage—or charges of mental cruelty. Privately, Simon confided that Veronika Clare was psychotic and he could prove it except that he didn't want the judge to think her unemployable and incapable of supporting herself.

Once the central themes of divorce trials, adultery and mental cruelty are now irrelevant under the law. In 1984 the Kellers were divorcing under the legal principle of no-fault, and officially, the court might or might not take moral issues into consideration when determining the value of the marital property and distributing it "equitably." But judges are human, and most lawyers believe that morality still counts, though now it is unofficial and must be sneaked in through the back door—in off-hand remarks that will be struck from the record, or under the guise of challenging the credibility of the spouse's testimony.

When I first started observing the Keller trial, Heinz was questioning Simon about his business records, trying to show that the defendant disguised his real income by charging to his new business (sensational, tabloid journalism) items that for others would be personal living expenses—a living room couch, steak dinners at the expensive Palm Restaurant, and $80 bills from Godiva Chocolatier. Simon had given up his original career as a serious actor to write scandal sheets about the rich and famous, and he claimed these furnishings and expenses were necessary to his business. Later that day, Mark Singer retaliated by showing that Veronika Clare took her own excessive tax deductions—in her last tax report she had doubled the rent figure she actually paid for her writing studio.

The court must be used to this. I once heard a judge dismiss a wife's complaints that her husband was lying by snapping, "So what? Everyone lies." According to divorce lawyers, most people are dishonest about money. If a couple has gone to trial over the division of property, chances are good the husband will try to hide his money, and what the wife gets depends on the tenacity of her lawyer. Simon had not bargained on a long trial. When he decided to go to court rather than settle with Veronika, it was because Singer told him a trial would take only a few days and Veronika would probably get very little.

The next day, Veronika Clare was telling the court why she had hardly worked for pay since marrying Simon in 1970. Before marrying him (at the time she was forty and he was twenty-seven), she had been a fairly successful opera singer, and though they never had children, Veronika worked only three months a year after marriage, when she taught summer-session singing classes. Her explanation for the change was that marriage to Simon was a full-time job. This was Veronika's refrain, her theme song throughout the trial. For a year after Simon left her, she was too traumatized to look for work. Then she was hired to coach singers in an off-Broadway play, but the producer fired her on the second day. Except for a fortuitous six-month consulting job for a cable television company, she had not worked during their three-year separation and had few prospects. A fifty-four-year-old singer who has been out of circulation for fourteen years is not exactly a hot property, she pointed out, and now she had diabetes, which further restricted her job prospects. In a rather strange appearance, Veronika's gynecologist was called to the stand to attest to this fact.

The judge presiding over the Keller trial was William Fox, a sixty-year-old small-town judge from upstate New York who had been assigned a month's tour of summer duty in Manhattan's Supreme Court. The world of the Kellers was foreign to him. When Veronika, going through her list of personal property articles, mentioned her Louis Vuitton designer luggage and her Cuisinart food processor, Judge Fox had to ask her to spell them. Lawyers say there are two kinds of judges: passive ones, who let the lawyers dominate, and judges who take control of a trial. Fox was clearly passive, which meant a longer trial. This did not please Simon Keller, who had fast-approaching deadlines for some of his projects. To Simon, the judge seemed like a cow that passes the day chewing cud.

After her gynecologist, Veronika's next witness was an attractive model who had double-dated with Simon and his new girl-friend, a woman twenty years younger than Veronika (he had moved in with Terry King three weeks after leaving Veronika). The model recounted Simon's dinner conversation about the house in fashionable East Hampton he shared with Ms. King in the summer months. Though Veronika intended the testimony to help paint a picture of Simon's high style of living, the point was largely lost on the judge in the swirl of flirtation surrounding the model's testimony. Smiling, and crossing and uncrossing her legs throughout the proceedings, she brought a foolish smile to Mark Singer's face as he cross-examined her. Even Judge Fox grinned. Veronika seemed not to notice.

During one of the many long breaks in the trial, Simon told me about the mutual torment in this marriage:

When I was married to Veronika, she couldn't stand it if I had a friend, male or female. She had to move in and take over every relationship. I married her when I was down. I was twenty-seven, and I had been a wunderkind in the theater outside New York, but when I came to Broadway, everything I tried was a commercial failure. I married Veronika because she was brilliant and strong, but over-

night she turned into a housewife and a bitch. She played
the seductress when we met, but after we married our sex
life was terrible. I knew it was a mistake the day I said "I
do." I went to a lawyer a week after the wedding to see if I
could get out of it, but he talked me out of annulling the
marriage. He said this happens to everyone, that I just
needed time to make an adjustment.

What did I know? I was a nice Jewish boy, and she was
already an angry woman. One thing I've learned is that
people with good marriages have good divorces and people
with bad marriages have bad divorces. I used to sit alone in
a friend's apartment, and just think about how wonderful it
would be just to be free of her. Every time I attempted to
leave her, she tried to kill herself—of course, she always
managed to miss the vein when she cut her wrists.

And don't worry about her; she's as strong as iron. And
all that strength is devoted to getting me. She once picked
up a 21-inch television and threw it at me. You should be
so strong. I wanted to leave her, but I felt sorry for her,
and I was afraid. I used to walk the streets, lonely and crying, until I went to a therapist to get the strength to leave
her. Now I'm about to remarry, and it's a joy to wake up in
the morning and see the face of a woman I love, though
she can't stand to hear about Veronika Clare anymore. All
Veronika cares about is destroying my life—she's had one
date in three years.

This time, when I marry, there will be a business contract. Marriage is a business—being in love only lasts a
short time. It upsets my girlfriend when I say this, but she
should understand; she has money of her own. She's only
thirty-three and already she's Miss Residential Real Estate
of New York, and she's making almost a hundred thousand
dollars a year.

On the eighteenth day of the trial, the lawyers met with a different judge to see if they could reach a settlement. During the
conference Simon spent the morning in the public telephone
booth in the corridor outside the courtroom, making a string of
calls to Los Angeles to try to gain extensions on his story deadlines.

While Simon made phone calls, Veronika paced around the empty courtroom. Heinz was starting to pressure her into settling for less than she wanted. I had observed that, sooner or later, this usually happened to the wives. While most of the husbands had the money to hire and fire lawyers as they wished, most of the wives had to settle for lawyers who were willing to take the case on retainers of five to ten thousand dollars. Then, when the lawyers figured they had already earned the maximum amount the judge would order the husband to pay them, they pressured the wife to settle.

Since Heinz was working on a salary he was more inclined to let Veronika's case drag on. But once the lawyers had disappeared into a bargaining session with the judge, Veronika started to panic. Alone (except for me) in the courtroom, she paced and cried, "It's all going too fast." Then she looked at me: "Simon and his girlfriend lived on five hundred thousand dollars last year, and I'm not going to wind up like a bag lady."

As she charged through the courtroom's swinging doors, Simon walked in, beaming:

> The judge we're negotiating with now is much better than
> Fox. He's cutting through all this crap, fast. That's why
> Veronika is so upset. Look at her. She's coming apart be-
> cause today she's a star, but tomorrow she's nobody. She
> has nothing to do. She just wants to go over the same pa-
> pers of mine, over and over again. I know it looks like I
> have a lot of money, but I'm in a high-expense business. I
> have a house in L.A. and an apartment in New York, and I
> have to travel back and forth. I have to entertain celebrities
> to pick up information and write my stories. If I had to
> liquidate my business today, I'd have nothing. It's true that
> I live well, but the main thing that's driving her crazy is
> two little words: Terry King. She can't stand it that I'm
> happy, and that I'm not under her thumb.

He left to see if Singer had emerged from the negotiations, and Veronika returned. Standing before the judge's bench she read aloud the words on the wall above, "In God We Trust." Then she crossed herself and turned to me. "Yesterday, one of the clerks told me, 'This is a court of law, not a court of justice.'

I can't be made a fool of, I can't." She rushed from the room, in tears.

When I returned an hour later, Veronika and Heinz were sitting alone in the courtroom, arguing. I sat in the back of the room, and they ignored me. Apparently, Simon had offered Veronika a $50,000 settlement on the marital property (mainly, the value of Simon's business) and Veronika wanted more. She doubted she would ever be able to collect any additional "maintenance" payments that might be awarded, and she wouldn't settle for less than $100,000 as her share of the marital property.

Heinz shook his head. "You're not going to get a hundred thousand."

"He has it. He could get a hundred thousand dollars in two hours."

"But he won't. You might as well take the fifty."

"But he spends more than fifty thousand dollars on two hookers and three lunches. He's a thief, a psychotic, a liar, a cheat. I'm being made a fool of."

"You made a fool of yourself the day you married Simon."

"He married me to use me. Now let him pay."

Heinz shrugged his shoulders. In the ensuing silence, a new, terrible thought must have crossed Veronika's mind.

"But with fifty thousand dollars, I'd be living on less than I've had during the separation."

"He doesn't have to give you as much as you've been getting. That's not the law."

"The law is just dollars and cents," she blurted.

"Of course. What else?"

Simon and Singer returned, and sat at the table. Talking to him for the first time in the trial, Veronika made a direct appeal. "Simon, you should be ashamed. Be fair, fair, fair—on your grandmother's life." Simon stared at her, and wordlessly stood up and headed for the door.

Veronika called after him. "Simon—twelve years."

"Of torture," he shouted back.

When the trial resumed, moments later, Veronika was still crying noisily. The kindly clerk asked if she wanted a cup of water. She snapped at him, "I'd like a cup of justice. If you can give me justice, I'll take it."

Singer, who was standing at the table, turned around and rolled his eyes upward, tucking his shirt into his pants as he waited impatiently.

Judge Fox was back and Simon returned to the witness stand, answering more questions about the same checks and bank statements they had been discussing for weeks. Furious, he kept slipping into the testimony remarks about how his business was going down the drain due to missed deadlines and cancelled interviews as the trial dragged on. Between every question and answer, Heinz took a long pause and shuffled through papers. Periodically, Singer would walk over to me and whisper that the case was killing him. Even though Simon was paying him two hundred fifty dollars an hour, he was neglecting other cases. While Heinz searched for a document, Singer begged the judge to give him twenty-five minutes to make a motion on behalf of another client in another courtroom in the building. Veronika protested they should adjourn for the day if Singer was leaving for twenty minutes. Singer screamed no, as he rushed out. Heinz approached the judge and complained, "Your Honor. Mr. Singer acts like he owns the courtroom in every case he takes." Without replying, Judge Fox rose and retired to his chambers.

To be fair to Singer, at one point, Heinz had taken fully twenty minutes to search through a messy pile of papers for a copy of a check he needed for his next question. Judge Fox meanwhile had sat motionless, staring at the back of the room. Finally, a bunch of papers fell from the table to the floor, and when Heinz stooped to retrieve them, he found what he was looking for. "It was underneath that stack," he explained, holding up the sheet of paper. Before asking his question, Heinz, still refusing to be hurried, performed his usual cross-examination ritual—first he removed his glasses, then he fished a dirty handkerchief from the pocket of his trousers and used it to polish first one lens and then another. Then he replaced the handkerchief and his glasses. He repeated the gesture again before asking each question. Simon stared at him from the witness stand; he'd already told me the thoughts that crossed his mind as he watched Heinz kill time: "I'd like to put my finger up through his nose and let it come out through his eye and hook his face and pull it away from his neck."

Later in the day, I asked Simon if it bothered him when his own lawyer, Singer, complained that the case was killing him. "Let him complain, I don't care. I've already paid him forty thousand dollars." Before hiring Singer, Simon had interviewed several lawyers and narrowed the choice to those with reputations as "killers." "At first I was impressed with how Mark could walk into the courtroom and snarl at Veronika, but then I watched him make an argument in another case and I saw him pulling the same act. You see, you just wind them up and they go. They're your gladiator for a high price."

It was a very different relationship from the kind I'd seen between wives and their lawyers. Having the money to hire and fire his lawyer at will, Simon had less cause to focus on their personalities or feel trapped and betrayed. The apparent equality in the relationship between Simon and his lawyer probably also stemmed from the fact that they had an affinity in their suspicion of women. In sharing a common enemy, they understood each other.

Simon was convinced that Veronika was using her professional skills to make herself look less employable. "Look at her, she painted her hair a drab color and she knows how to lay on the makeup to make herself look older. She knows just how to dress like the poor little match girl."

I asked about her former career. "By the time I met her, she wasn't singing anymore. By the time you're forty, if you haven't made it as a singer, your career is finished. She doesn't really have connections in the theater anymore."

Simon's star had faded also. After he failed to have any commercial success as an actor, he drifted into writing and publishing sensational journalism about politicians and movie stars. In the last few years he had started to make more money by giving up any serious artistic aspirations. One of the disputes of the trial concerned the value of one of his tabloid stories for resale to broadcast television. Simon maintained it had far too many legal problems to be used for network television, while Veronika insisted there was a market for it. The next witness for the defense, a television executive, supported Simon's claims that his work could never be sold to television.

As the days passed in testimony over the value of the property and Veronika's prospects for work, Simon told me more about his marriage:

I went into a therapy group to find out why I couldn't leave Veronika, and the whole group was made up of strong women and weak men. My father was a business failure, and the only thing that counted in my house was being a business success. When I was four, and playing under the kitchen table, my mother said to me in front of my father, "You better work hard, or you'll wind up like him." My father was a weak man. He promised me there would be money to help me go to Yale, but a few days before I was supposed to leave, he told me he had lied. So I went to Brooklyn College, and because of my father I've never had any respect for male authority.

He nodded to Veronika, who was seated at the table, turning pages:

Look at her, going through the checks, over and over, like Madame De Farge. What's she gonna find there? There's nothing. She used to search through my pockets, looking for phone numbers of women, so I used to plant numbers there as decoys, or numbers to upset her, like the Suicide Center.

In the fifth week of the trial, Heinz put himself on the stand to testify that his employer had informally promised him $55,000 for his pretrial and trial work. (This had to be figured in, since Simon would be responsible for paying both lawyers.) Singer, furious at the way the case had been handled, established that this was Heinz's first matrimonial case. Then, with a flourish, he produced a document in which Heinz's employer had agreed that Heinz's salary would be fixed by the court, contrary to Heinz's $55,000 understanding. Still enraged by what he regarded as his adversary's incompetence, he asked, "Mr. Heinz, will you tell us why you don't take notes in court?"

"Because I store important information in my memory."

"Will you tell us, where are your pretrial notes?"

Heinz replied that he had none, and asked why he had to answer this line of questioning.

"Your honor," bellowed Singer. "The answer is so obvious, but I'll spell it out. Mr. Heinz says that he wants twenty-six thousand dollars for his pretrial work, but I'm demonstrating that we were forced to compel every act from his office, that they were guilty of heel-dragging in the worst sense, that there was plenty of time for the pretrial discovery but instead of doing work when he should have, Mr. Heinz has taken an unbelievable amount of time from this court. I'm not sure he should be paid at all."

In the afternoon, Simon returned to the stand to identify the personal property he had left in the marital apartment and to give it a value. He had prepared a thorough list, but now, searching through his briefcase, he couldn't find it. He looked imploringly at the judge.

"Do it from memory," Mark prompted.

"I don't want to leave anything out." He continued to search through his briefcase. "I can't find it." He looked up in despair.

Veronika was laughing, for the first time in weeks, and Singer looked unsympathetic.

"O.K. I'll do it from memory," Simon agreed, looking unhappy.

"Just think carefully," Singer encouraged. "Visualize."

"A wing chair—it's worth three hundred dollars." Veronika laughed. "The sofa in the living room—it's worth eight or nine hundred dollars." Veronika gave a hoot.

"I don't want to go through each item and have Miss Clare jump up and down and make noises," he complained to Fox.

"Just don't look at her," urged Singer. "What else?"

"Two solid gold pendants I had made at Tiffany's; each had Scorpio and Libra signs. They're both the same, and one is mine."

"Whose is the other?" asked Judge Fox, who was making a list.

"Miss Clare's."

"Mrs. Keller," Veronika called out.

"You never used that name during the marriage."

"What else?"

"My father's knives. My father was a butcher and my mother gave me these particular knives that were his."

"What else?"

"My awards and memorabilia from college. Articles I wrote, and articles written about me. My file cabinet and its contents, including my therapy notes."

Singer shifted the topic. "Did there ever come a time after you were married when you discussed with the plaintiff the subject of her employment?"

Yes. From a year after we were married. When I saw she wasn't looking for singing and coaching work. When work was offered to her and she turned it down. At first I thought that she wanted to set up house. Then I asked her, carefully, why she wasn't working. She accused me of being mercenary and philistine. She'd say, "Now I'm a writer." And I said, "If you're a writer, go sell your work." She said, "I pay for the office," and I said, "Fine, you have an office, and have lunches and teas, but I don't see why I should have to support you for the rest of your life." She took writing courses. She fixed up her office. She did all the preparation, but she didn't write anything. Prior to the marriage we discussed having children. I said I didn't want any, emphatically. She said she didn't want them either, and she was beyond child-bearing age anyway.

It was four o'clock on Wednesday, in the fifth week of the trial, and Judge Fox announced that since he had to go upstate for two days, he was adjourning the trial until 9:30 A.M. the following Monday.

Shocked by the news of the delay, and distraught with self-pity because his uncompleted projects were being cancelled, Simon began to cry, and Singer begged the judge to keep going that afternoon.

The judge refused, adding that it would take them more than one hour to finish the trial anyway.

"Guaranteed," chimed Heinz, delighted.

"I'll sue the state for harassment," Simon threatened the judge. He had to be in California over the weekend, and he hadn't planned to return on Monday.

Veronika turned around toward me and commented on the new delay. "I feel sorry for his lawyer, but not for Simon. He's losing his business? Let him settle. Let him take the money from his girlfriend, the way he took it from me."

Simon did not go to California that weekend. When I saw him on Monday morning he skipped the customary greetings. "It's not fair. I never did anything to deserve this. I never felt so impotent in all my life."

Heinz was back on his theme of a fraudulent property transfer. It was his argument that Simon was lying when he testified that he was no longer in business with a former partner, a Jerry Roberts, and was lying when he testified that he had sold Roberts all his rights to a publication for $15,000. To prove that Simon was still really in business with his former partner, Heinz produced a page from the New York telephone directory that listed Simon at Roberts' work number.

"Your honor," objected Singer. "I once said that counsel for the plaintiff had introduced everything into evidence but the phone book, and now I stand corrected. This is highly irregular as evidence."

But Heinz had one more surprise. "Mr. Keller, didn't you testify that the plaintiff doesn't deserve a penny?"

"Yes."

He showed Simon some notes. "Are these written in your hand?" Simon nodded and looked imploringly at Singer.

Mr. Keller, did you write these words: 'She gave me a kind of status and power by introducing me to people in show business'?"

"Not in my right mind, I didn't. You're reading from notes I made under a doctor's care. I refuse to answer."

"Did you write those words, yes or no?"

Now Singer was on his feet and shouting, "You should be ashamed." Heinz was shouting back.

The judge ordered them both into his chambers. Simon stepped down from the stand and sat quietly at his end of the table. Veronika leafed through papers.

I stepped into the corridor and Simon joined me, telling me that when he went into Fisher-Hoffman therapy to find the strength to leave Veronika, he was instructed to write intensively of all his feelings of guilt and hatred, taking everything to the limit. When he left Veronika, he left the notes behind in a locked file cabinet in their apartment.

Fox and the lawyers returned and Simon was back on the stand. Heinz held up another portion of the notes and read: "Veronika, I married you for all the wrong reasons. I was always duplicitous. . . . Donna is twenty-five. She left her husband for me when I knew I'd never marry her. She's really angry with me, as is Karen. She wanted me to leave Veronika, and I sort of said I would. She hung around 'til she got tired of it and dumped me."

When Singer objected, Heinz argued the documents were relevant to show that Simon's veracity was in doubt: "Who can believe a self-confessed liar and exploiter who married his wife because she could help his career?"

"Your honor," Singer objected. "The court should be dealing with reality, and not with the workings of someone's mind. This is a terrible invasion of privacy."

Heinz read on. "Veronika, I have been duplicitous and dishonest with you. I was never to be trusted. I never gave you the love and understanding you deserved." He turned a page. "Well, it hasn't been all bad. Veronika's a great woman and a great influence. We owe a great deal of our taste to her—so if our sex life isn't the greatest, so what? Do you know how much of our lives we owe to Veronika? How loving and caring she is? You should be ashamed." He looked at Simon. "Did you write this, Mr. Keller?"

"It was an exercise, an internal dialogue. You're taking it out of context. I was supposed to look at myself as a prosecutor, to bring my demons to the surface."

Heinz fingered still another twenty-nine pages and asked Simon if they were in his handwriting.

Simon looked and smiling wearily shook his head, yes.

"Your honor, I suggest you read these in private." Heinz handed the pages to the judge.

There was still honor among men. Simon later told me that this section was called "My Sexual Failures Before and During Marriage."

After handing the notes to the judge, Heinz gathered a copy for Singer's inspection, but somehow managed to drop them, and the twenty-nine sheets scattered all over the floor. He bent over with exertion, scooped them up, and handed the pages to Singer.

"Are these in order, Mr. Heinz?"

"They're numbered, you can count as easily as I can."

"I didn't drop them on the floor."

Singer objected to this portion, as he had to all portions, of the therapy notes going into evidence. "Your honor, you're supposed to weigh facts, not interpret dreams or fantasies. The facts are in—what money he has, what he doesn't have. The financial evidence they produce and what we produce is the same, and it's all in the record."

With that, Singer tried to return the notes to Simon, but Heinz interfered, giving them instead to Veronika. "Mr. Keller abandoned his house and property. They belong to Mrs. Keller now."

Fifty years ago, the German philosopher Theodor Adorno, writing about divorce, observed that the unwatchful trust of shared life is transformed into a malignant poison as soon as a marriage is broken off. Even Veronika must have felt uneasy about using the therapy notes, because that afternoon when she passed me in the corridor outside the courtroom, she rationalized the betrayal. "He once left the notes on the kitchen table so I'd see them. He had a key. He could have come back and gotten the notes whenever he wanted to. He meant for me to see them."

By the end of the day, there was nothing to add. Judge Fox informed Singer and Heinz that they'd each have one hour the next day for their closing arguments. Simon whispered something to Singer and Singer stood and announced that since the defendant was no longer needed for testimony, he was leaving immediately for California.

The next morning, Simon's absence dominated the courtroom. Even Veronika's bitter alertness seemed to go slack without his presence. Singer's summary came first. He went through the facts as he saw them, what money there was and what money there wasn't. Then he turned to his "theme" for the case:

> Your honor, last night, when I was working late, I sent out to the Chinese restaurant for my dinner, and after I had my spare ribs I opened my fortune cookie and it said, "You get out of life what you put in." [Veronika turned around and smiled at me, to underscore his triteness.]
>
> You get as much as you give. Veronika has no debts. Her savings have grown in recent years. Let's look at her budget. She says she needs two hundred dollars a week for food. But she doesn't eat breakfast, she hardly eats lunch, and she gets invited out for dinner a lot. She made a big, big deal about being only four feet ten-and-a half inches tall when she claimed she can't get a singing job. Well, unless she eats only caviar she couldn't eat two hundred dollars worth of food every week.
>
> Sure, if a woman gives up thirty years of her life to have children, sure, you have to support her for longer. But with a childless woman who got married for just ten years when she was already forty, who had contacts in the theater and has kept them up, she has no right to support.

She's already had three years of it. There's got to be a time when the defendant doesn't have to keep paying and paying. She regards what's hers as hers and what's his as hers. This woman should not be allowed to lead her life as a dilettante. I'm not, and you're not.

After lunch, Heinz had his hour and ended on a moral note:

Mr. Keller goes around the world on company expense with his girlfriend, but that doesn't mean that Mrs. Keller doesn't have to eat or dress. If your honor believes, as he shouldn't, that Mr. Keller transferred his publication rights for a few thousand dollars, then he should consider this wasteful dissipation of property and your honor should increase the maintenance payments as compensation.

As for Mrs. Keller's contribution to the business, I quote Mr. Keller from his own writing: "She gave me a kind of power and status and access to the key people in show business." He also refers to how she gave him "class"—your honor, we must consider the circles she traveled in, the class she gave him, as what she contributed to the career potential of this butcher's son.

There is one other thing Mr. Singer said to which I agree. He said you can't get something for nothing. Mr. Keller had a wife, he had a wife he used, he had a wife he cast aside and abandoned with no cause. He can't say I owe her nothing and get away with this. That is not equity or justice.

While Singer and Heinz packed their documents, Veronika and I had our final conversation. With Simon absent, she had the last word:

I never cared about money—I married Simon because he was creative. I married him because of his potential—I'm a teacher. We were going to be a team—the theater is so competitive, the only people who make it are those who work in pairs.

I wanted to have a child, and when I couldn't I wanted to adopt a Vietnamese child or a child with a handicap, but

Simon wanted to be the child. You can see from his therapy notes how immature and infantile he is—he's completely cut off from his feelings. There's no center there. I was going to help him put it all together.

Look what he's produced since he left me—Grade D garbage. He's a Grade D journalist. I was Grade A, with Grade A contacts. He takes short cuts—that's why he gets fired all the time. I could ruin him today, by making just two phone calls. That's why he couldn't stand me—I made him feel like a failure. He had to have someone who isn't a threat, a woman like Terry King who sells real estate.

He's much more materialistic than I am—he needs money to boost his ego. When he left me, he left behind ten pairs of shoes and fifteen suits in the closet. [I had heard about these suits before—Simon told me Veronika cut them to shreds.] He's all show. The first thing he came back for was his tuxedo. He gave a Christmas part at Terry King's house right after he left me and invited all our friends.

These men have no inner sense of themselves so they need the external signs of success—the woman on their arm and a wad of money in their pocket. I'm sure if you asked Simon for a dollar he'd produce a thick wad of bills. He always carries around hundreds of dollars. I feel sorry for him. He's been in a midlife crisis and I think he still is. I'd still help him if he were ever in need, because I remember why I loved him. In a way, Terry King doesn't count—she's irrelevant. Simon and I saw each other a few times after he left me, and he told me he was bored to death with her. He won't remarry unless he does it tomorrow. He's still wrapped up in me, angry with me for things that go back to his early life—I just became the receptacle for his anger.

Veronika was not alone among the wives I met in court who had fantasies of opening their doors, years hence, to a repentant ex-husband. Like an animal mother in the wild standing guard over the carcass of a lost baby, these women could not desert their posts, even long after their ministrations ceased to serve any function.

When Simon married Veronika he married a mother who would make him a success, as his real mother wouldn't do for his father. Even more than a woman with contacts, Simon married a woman he admired who believed in him, a woman who would hold up a flattering image of himself. For this husband, as for many, love meant looking upward to a woman who gazed down with adoration.

When Veronika married, she sought redemption too, but through a lover-son who would throw garlands at her feet. At forty, she had come to the end of her career as a singer and her chance to have a baby. For Veronika, marriage to Simon signified the transfer of narcissism from the aging performer to the young performer. She had no future, but he did. She could no longer believe in her own status, so like many wives, she set up her young husband to carry her banner.

As long as he succeeded, they were both redeemed. But when Simon fell short of their joint expectations, the pair could no longer sustain the inflated image of him, and Simon heard the deepening echoes of his mother's comments about his father. A wife's ironic comments about her husband's inadequacies express the underside of patriarchal marriage, Adorno observed. As he noted, there is hardly a woman who doesn't disavow her husband by whispering about his little weaknesses. His power rests on his capacity to make money which is "trumped up as human worth," while her power rests on deflating him: "The whole sombre base on which the institution of marriage rises, the husband's barbarous power over the property and work of his wife, the no less barbarous sexual oppression that can compel a man to take life-long responsibility for a woman with whom it once gave him pleasure to sleep—all this crawls into the light from cellars and foundations when the house is demolished."[1]

Eventually, Veronika's ironic remarks become those Simon had first heard directed against his father as he played under the table when he was four. He was infantile, a failure, and impotent with this angry woman who held him in contempt. The beacon of light she had once gleamed upon him had now become an ugly glare.

No one can hold up under the criticism of a person who is admired, and Simon started out in life weakened by the hatred between his parents. Redeemers often turn into destroyers, and though Veronika Clare started out making Simon feel strong, she ended up making him feel worthless. The man who was once a promising actor now enacted his humiliation by publishing trivia and gossip. Simon was the poor butcher's son, but it's the frustrated wives who sharpen the knives. When he asked the court for his father's knives, Simon wanted the blades that had castrated his father and himself.

As Veronika knew, Simon hated his mother in his own name and in his father's, and he used his wife as a target after first using her to redeem him. But in coaching Simon to act for them both, Veronika had prepared her own downfall as well as her husband's.

The court of divorce no longer makes monetary awards for pain and suffering, though that is the logic that husbands and wives are driven by. Like victims of medical negligence who sue over lost limbs, the wounded survivors of marriage seek, in the language of the law, to be "made whole." And why not? In a world where money is the measure of all value, every value ought to be convertible into a sum. As surely as the value of Mr. Keller's business was Mr. Keller himself, so was Veronika's case built on the proposition that she was as marketable as an old rag. A woman of fifty-four commands a low price in the world of love and world of work, while Simon was still a valuable commodity.

It's ironic that both Simon and Veronika have known much greater happiness in their professional lives than in their personal lives, despite the fact that their stars have faded. The obvious competitiveness of commercial culture had forced them to be realistic about their professions and still find a way to make a living doing the work they loved. Those who choose to work in the arts must face the commercial realities. But, as Adorno observed, it's only after the house of marriage collapses in divorce that people can see the financial foundation that was there all along. In business, we have rules and contracts that force people to be realistic about their work and thus find some happiness in it. If only we could do this for love and the family, people like Simon and Veronika might not fall into such personal disaster.

It would be satisfying to tell how the case of *Keller* v. *Keller* turned out. But like the endless lawsuit in Dickens's novel *Bleak House*, a contest that dragged on for generations, taking everyone with it, the case of the Kellers has never reached an end. Just months after Judge Fox announced his decision for dividing the marital property, Veronika discovered new evidence, and when I last looked at the court calendar, the pair was scheduled for another appearance. Like Dickens's characters, Simon and Veronika still live in a state of perpetual postponement, waiting for the justice and the peace of a settlement that eludes them.

10

———•———

The Work of Love

*I*t is often still true that men live for work, and women live for
love. In her reflections on the different meanings of love for
men and women (written in 1949), Simone de Beauvoir began
with Nietzsche's memorable description:

> The single word love in fact signifies two different things
> for man and woman. What woman understands by love is
> clear enough: it is not only devotion, it is a total gift of
> body and soul, without reservation, without regard for any-
> thing whatever. This unconditional nature of her love is
> what makes it a *faith*, the only one she has. As for man, if
> he loves a woman, what he *wants* is that love from her; he
> is in consequence far from postulating the same sentiment
> for himself as for woman; if there should be men who also
> felt that desire for complete abandonment, upon my word,
> they would not be men."[1]

Searching for the source of the difference, Simone de Beauvoir
argued that a woman's subordinate position in the world compels
her to become a slave of love, a worshipper of the god she fash-
ions out of love: "She chooses to desire her enslavement so ardently that it will seem to her the expression of her liberty. . . .
Love becomes for her a religion."[2]

But perhaps that faith and devotion in love are not really the
antithesis of men's involvement in work, but another kind of occupation? Many have observed that women's love for men provides the underpinnings of male accomplishments. Yet love may

133

not only be the hidden foundation for the work of others, but a career in itself, learned and practiced like any other profession.

Arlie Hochschild, a sociologist, makes a compelling argument about love as work: like other emotions, love is not simply left to impulse. According to Hochschild, whenever we feel an emotion, whether it is love, anger, sadness, or jealousy, we don't merely surrender to the emotion, we manage it. Whenever we have a feeling, we hold it up to a standard of what we think we should be feeling, a standard that is culturally prescribed for our gender and class. Always comparing our feeling to our sense of what we should be feeling, we bridge the gap by working at our emotions—inducing, suppressing, and refining them like Stanislavskian actors. The person who would fight off love for a former spouse, for example, might deliberately call up memories of old hurts and grievances to gain that end. According to Hochschild's theory, feelings don't happen naturally, they are produced through tremendous effort and shaped by social conventions.

Hochschild suggests there are class, occupational, and gender differences in our propensity to "work" on our emotions, and that it's done more by women than men. The differences in our readiness to do "emotion work" are not only learned but structural. Because women lack money, power, and status, they have to use emotions as a resource in the marketplace, trading good feelings for financial support. Emotions are a woman's capital—they're what she works with, invests in, spends, and manipulates, the assets she uses to deal with other people. As a result, not only are middle-class American women presumed to feel emotion more than men, but women are also perceived as being more skilled in managing emotions: "to command 'feminine wiles,' to have the capacity to premeditate a sigh, an outburst of tears, or a flight of joy."[3] Leaving aside the problem of how one may distinguish a spontaneous feeling from a willfully managed one, Hochschild argues that women, depending on men for money, repay their debt in part by doing extra emotion work, "especially emotion work that affirms, enhances, and celebrates the well-being and status of others."[4]

Can emotional support given for a price be genuine or truly comforting to the buyer? Some might think not, but in our society we are used to paying for emotional support. If one pays a therapist for attention, why not a wife?

According to Hochschild, the reliance on emotion as an asset that can be exchanged is not intrinsically related to gender. It's associated with subordination. Being understanding, being sensitive, making the other person feel good, even putting that person's emotional needs before one's own—these are traits not narrowly confined to women. They are strategies common to all categories of people in subordinate positions, including blacks and homosexuals, and white, heterosexual men married to higher-class women. But in the case of women, the structural pressure to please the person on whom one depends also combines with other cultural influences to produce an individual who will work endlessly to suppress her own anger or doubts and to keep pouring out love, understanding, and encouragement.

Hochschild's argument explains why so many women who appear on these pages speak of the work of love, and why their expectation for compensation has a certain logic. One woman, divorcing a clinically depressed husband, claims she earned a share of his inheritance because she kept him sane and functioning over many years. Another woman, dumped by her husband, argues in court that she deserves half of the marital property, though she didn't work for wages, because her husband was a "full-time job." The perspective on marriage changes with divorce: going into marriage, people think of the union primarily in terms of love. Going out, they see it in terms of money. Similarly, as long as people are embedded in a relationship, they see their emotional efforts as love. When the relationship dissolves, what was understood as love, in retrospect, turns out to have been labor.

If love has become women's work in modern times, the origins must be traced to changes in economic arrangements. It is generally agreed among social historians that the modern family, experienced as a private world separated from public life and as a place of intimate relationships, came into full flowering only in the nineteenth century. Once industrialization separated most families from the ownership of productive property, "work" and "personal life" were increasingly separated. Just as capitalist development gave rise to the idea of the family as a realm separate from the economy, so did it create a separate sphere of "personal" life where people could experience and express their authentic selves.

As the workplace became more impersonal, the family became the place where people were to be valued in themselves. But the new division between the public and private spheres also separated women from men, and produced a more dichotomized view of manhood and womanhood, a more elaborate scheme of sex roles. It also made women's positions more precarious as men worked for wages and women performed the unpaid and increasingly devalued work at home. With this new conception of the family as the refuge from the competitive world came a related development: the modern conceptions of children and childrearing.

In earlier times, European and North American children had mingled freely with adults and were less differentiated from them. There was little conception of "childhood" or "adolescence" as distinct stages of life with special psychological needs. According to Christopher Lasch and other social historians, with the development of the modern family, children were increasingly viewed as different from adults—unformed and vulnerable, in need of a long, protective period of nurture. The nineteenth century woman was expected to serve not only as an "angel of consolation" to her husband when he returned from the brutal workplace, but as the patient nurturer of the children, who increasingly became the center of middle-class family life.[5]

The sentimentalized notion of the family as a refuge from the cruel world reached its fullest expression in the Victorian period. The home, wrote John Ruskin, was "the place of peace; the shelter, not only from all injury, but from all terror, doubt, and division."[6] Like many other social critics of the time, Ruskin feared that without the family and female influence, the market would destroy all human bonds.

The idea that women have a distinct morality that resists the values of the marketplace became widely accepted, and it is still popular with social scientists and philosophers. It was one of the arguments used by nineteenth century suffragists who believed women should be given the vote because they would raise public moral standards and conduct. Even today there are many who believe that women must save the world from the allegedly male values that have brought us to the brink of nuclear destruction.[7]

Although the concept has a certain appeal, in that it turns women's traditional weaknesses (noncompetitiveness, for example)

into virtues, it's important to bear in mind what Elizabeth Janeway
has said about the "powers of the weak." Janeway argues that just
as we tend to glamourize the authority of the powerful, we often
sentimentalize the powerless, projecting onto females, for example, certain virtues (like being loving, warm, supportive) and
thereby falsifying their true position: "But when our mythology
instructs any class of adults that it is their role to be gentler and
more virtuous or humbler than the powerful, it operates as a form
of social control."[8]

In fact, most of the social dichotomies we have created around
gender and money are false. They represent our attempts as individuals and societies to deal with the ambivalence and conflicts
we have about merging and separating. There is a false duality
projected on to gender that attempts to solve the conflicting pulls
we feel between the mind and body, reason and emotion, the
individual and the community. One way to deal with conflict,
including conflict between the wish to connect and join with others and the wish to be autonomous and separate, is to attribute
different sides of the conflict to men and women.

Love, as we understand it in our culture, requires us to sacrifice
a certain measure of autonomy and control. To love is to be vulnerable. Love is the symbol of connection, it is the sticky stuff that
keeps us tied to one another. Money is the symbol of separation—
it is the basis of autonomy, and it buys us freedom. We see these
as polar opposites, and they are. Yet all of us have conflicts about
separation and connection, and we misrepresent the real world
when we project these into false dualities like male and female,
love and money, family and marketplace.

The idea that the family protects us from the corruption of the
marketplace and that Victorian domestic values resist those of the
marketplace are still popular and dearly held beliefs. Today, feminists are being attacked for not defending and supporting the
traditional family. According to neoconservatives and now, even
some voices from the left, such as the historian, Christopher
Lasch, it's the fault of the women's movement that the family has
been weakened and made vulnerable to the infiltration and corruption of consumerism and the public realm.

In two influential books,[9] Lasch attacked feminism for viewing
the family as oppressive to women because it prevents them from
competing and gaining equality with men in the world of jobs and

careers. In Lasch's view, feminists' ideas of emancipated woman-hood reflect the selfishness and narcissism of the "me-decade" as well as the excessive individual self-aggrandizement bred by capitalism. Blaming women for abandoning their children to inadequate day care centers so they, the mothers, can get ahead, he sentimentalizes the traditional family of breadwinner father and homemaker mother as the vanishing source of values for resisting the corruptions of a capitalist-industrial system. According to Lasch, the decline of the traditional patriarchal family has produced a culture that is narcissistic and psychologically driven to buying and consuming.

Lasch's attack on feminism as the source of family problems is both mistaken and misleading. Lasch would have us think that women have gone to work not because they and their families need the money to survive but rather out of personal ambition and because they don't care enough about their children. He says,

> The trouble with the feminist program, is not that economic self-sufficiency for women is an unworthy goal but that its realization, under existing economic conditions, would undermine equally important values associated with the family. . . . Feminists have not answered the argument that day care provides no substitute for the family. They have not answered the argument that indifference to the needs of the young has become one of the distinguishing characteristics of a society that lives for the moment, defines the consumption of commodities as the highest form of personal satisfaction, and exploits existing resources with criminal disregard of the future.[10]

I mention Lasch's argument because there are echoes of it in many popular views of our current domestic troubles. The women's movement with its emphasis on economic independence and equality for women is often blamed for the high divorce rates and the alleged deterioration of youth and family life. But feminist scholars have uncovered a different portrait of the traditional family. As sociologist Barrie Thorne has argued,[11] the nineteenth-century traditional family whose passing Lasch regrets was a fictive one in many respects. Women's and men's real experiences of the family have been obscured not only by the sentimentalization of motherhood but also by portraying the "companionate marriage" of the modern family as based on love and equality.

In recent years, feminists have tried to correct the sentimentalized view of the traditional family by emphasizing the inequalities, domination, conflicts of interest, and even widespread violence that are as much a part of family as love and sharing. As Thorne points out, a closer examination shows that the home is not a refuge—a nurturing haven—for all, but only for some:

> For men, who do far less housework than women, the
> home indeed may be experienced as a refuge, or at least a
> place of considerable leisure. But for almost all women, the
> home is a place of considerable work. Time budget studies
> reveal a consistent pattern of women doing much more
> housework than men. Wives with full-time employment put
> in an additional 26 to 35 hours a week doing housework.
> Their husbands do the same or only slightly more
> housework—averaging between 10 and 14 hours a week—
> than men whose wives are full-time housekeepers.[12]

While "pro-family" political movements cling to an image of the traditional family, in fact only a minority of family households resemble the sentimentalized form. As everyone knows, the transformation in the composition of households has been going on for some time. Thorne reports that even in 1977, only 16 percent of all U.S. households included a father as sole wage earner, a full-time homemaker mother, and at least one child living at home. In another 18 percent of all households, both parents were wage earners, while 30 percent included married couples with no children at home, and 6 percent were single-parent families headed by women; another 21 percent were composed of single people living alone.[13] Recent figures on the percentage of mothers in the workforce also attest to the collapse of the traditional family of the nineteenth century. Today, 72 percent of married women with school-age children work outside the home. These women are not in the workforce because they are narcissistic or have no concern for their children, as Lasch suggests. They're working because they need to support their families.

The sentimental view of the family as a haven has been questioned on other grounds as well. When antifeminists attacked the

Equal Rights Amendment, their rhetoric played on the anticipated loss of the nurturant, intimate bonds we associate with the family.[14] Yet both social histories of the family and any current newspaper with daily reports of family violence and child abuse should remind us that people do not always find nurture and support in the family.[15]

One of the most interesting replies to the blame that's been heaped on the women's movement for the break-up of the family comes from Barbara Ehrenreich, who discovered a prior "male revolt" against the breadwinner role. Ehrenreich argues that long before the revival of American feminism in the late 60s and 70s, men had already begun to rebel against the traditional expectation that a healthy, adult man is one who is married and supporting a family.

Beginning in the 1950s, the old view of the breadwinner role as a requirement of masculinity was starting to erode, according to Ehrenreich, and by the 1970s, expert opinion, popular culture, and popular psychology were all shifting to offer an image of manhood that did not require supporting a family. According to Ehrenreich, today's man "who postpones marriage even into middle age, who avoids women who are likely to become financial dependents, who is dedicated to his own pleasures, is likely to be found not suspiciously deviant, but 'healthy'."[16] What Ehrenreich documents so amusingly is that while for the man of the 1950s, a family and a mortgage were viewed as the markers of maturity, by the 1970s popular psychology placed the seal of psychological health on the man who is physically fit and self-assertive enough to be free of unwanted dependents and happy to "do his own thing."

Unfortunately, the collapse of the male breadwinner ethic has contributed to the chaos in an economic system based on the principle of the family wage. As Ehrenreich argued, the American economy was based on the principle that a male worker should be paid enough to support a family. Men are still greatly favored in the labor market where they earn, on average, 40 percent more than women, and this pattern does not seem to be changing. But, today, nothing compels men to share their "family wages" with women and children. After divorce, less than half of the women who are awarded child support by the courts actually get all of it, and most receive only minimal payments.[17]

The cultural ideologies that shape our ideas and moral expectations about love and adulthood are indeed changing, not only for men but for women, and they are intertwined with changes in the economic realities of people's lives. In a time when most marriages were permanent and relationships stable, the differentiation of male and female roles and a "family wage" system that paid men more still allowed for the support of families even though they subordinated women and made them dependent. A division of labor and a division of gender were still somewhat workable for families as long as everyone was locked into the relationships and responsible for them. But now that marriages are unstable and relationships more temporary, the division of labor and gender and a wage system that pays men more has become catastrophic for women and children. In a society where relationships are temporary and where people must be able to rely on themselves, both men and women have to be self-sufficient and autonomous, emotionally and financially. A system based on making different contributions doesn't work when the ties aren't enduring.

Not surprisingly, our culture increasingly emphasizes the importance of personal growth as a continuous process, and defines mental health in terms of being adaptable and able to survive change and loss, of being autonomous enough to travel alone. Being autonomous also requires dispensing with gender distinctions: to be able to make it alone, each person must be equipped with the emotional and practical capacities that were formerly divided and shared.

Sociologist Ann Swidler has examined this shift in beliefs about what is a healthy adult, and points out that the modern emphasis on "self-actualization" and continuing change and growth in adulthood places more value on being able to choose freely than on commitment. The ideology of love, she argues, has radically shifted. Where once a person consolidated an identity through a one-time choice and commitment to a life-long partner, today we no longer speak of "true love" as a love we would die for, or die without. Rather we talk of love that is "meaningful" or "alive," because it involves "honesty" and it stimulates us to discover ourselves and to change.

According to Swidler's argument, love relationships today are judged less by the degree of commitment they display than by what they contribute to self-development. Previously, a love that ended was viewed as a failure, but today people speak of what they have gained or learned or taken away from relationships that have ended:

> Each person can grow and learn, even from loss and disappointment. Indeed permanence, which was the hallmark of success in the earlier model of identity formation, becomes almost a sign of failure. After all, is it that likely that one can keep growing and changing with the same partner? . . . The greatest sin a lover can commit is not betrayal, reneging on a commitment, but obstruction, trying to thwart, hamper, or limit another's freedom to grow.[18]

Swidler sees the shift in love ideology as necessarily related to a shift in how people achieve an identity in work. In a highly mobile society like our own, no membership in any particular social world can adequately provide a stable sense of identity. Therefore, work on the "self" becomes the most important form of work. In a society some would call narcissistic, the self becomes one's major form of capital. Even though modern life increasingly separates the realms of emotion and work, Swidler argues that in other ways, love and work have become fused. In our culture, they have both become problems of the "restless self," the self that must be kept unfettered, flexible, and ready to change.

One pattern she sees in the new, popular view of love and work "turns love itself into a kind of work. For some people in modern society the continual negotiation and renegotiation of personal relationships becomes the major sphere of accomplishment in daily life. People take on 'struggle' in their relationships with a vengeance."[19]

Love and work have converged, also, in the reliance on a contract that leaves nothing to chance. Swidler observes that since we value autonomy and independence above all else, relationships are now required to be explicitly articulated so that "no tentacles of unrecognized attachment can reach out to strangle, no illegitimate expectations can develop."[20] The current propensity for bargaining over every specific term gives some protection and a way out, since people need only be bound to what they agreed to: "Good lovers, like good workers, cannot afford unlimited attachments. They may stay on, but only if the terms are right, if the job or relationship permits them continued development."[21]

Though some may find it sad that anyone should have to submit love to this kind of bargaining, there's a trend in this direction and it has a logic. The high divorce rate has forced people to think of marriage as not necessarily permanent, and with that comes the need to be clearer about terms, conditions, and procedures. Since people are marrying when they're older and more likely to have assets, or more than once and when they have children from a previous marriage, they need a contract for clarifying obligations and dividing property in the event of divorce. A growing number of gay and lesbian couples who have shared a household or raised children together are also getting into expensive lawsuits when they break up and have to divide their property. They need contracts most of all because since the state doesn't recognize their union, they don't even have the protection provided by state marital laws.

Prenuptial and nuptial contracts are financially advantageous because the legal costs of disputed divorces have become so immense they can eat up all the marital assets, as they did in the case of the Kellers. And in some ways, clear contracts are emotionally advantageous because although they're unromantic and bruise some illusions, they also provide useful boundaries in expectations and dependence and force people to think more deliberately and realistically about money and relationships. According to Raoul Felder, a prominent New York matrimonial lawyer, people can't afford to marry without an agreement—they're the "wave of the future. Everybody should have one."[22]

In 1986, the *New York Times*[23] ran a story about this new trend, and presented the case of a man who, taken to the cleaners on his last divorce, was insisting on a contract now that he was remarrying. His proposed contract spelled out what he'd have to pay his wife if they divorced and read "almost like a corporate vesting plan, in that the amount of alimony he would pay goes up with each year the marriage lasts." According to the *Times*, the man said he would have allowed his real name to be used in the article, except that his fiancée was "angry and embarrassed" by the agreement.

Many people who are made to sign a contract as a condition of marriage feel embarrassed or humiliated because it reveals that they have less power in the relationship and because it puts a discounted price tag on their love. But love is never really unconditional, and in the long run, it helps to have a realistic view of the partnership one is entering. When both partners are capable of financial independence, the notion of a contract is less embarrassing—then it's not a matter of exploitation or show of power but merely a matter of being clear and businesslike. Ideally, *this* will be the wave of the future for prenuptial contracts, rather than their use to pay a cheap price for a disposable partner.

The more frequent appearance of formal business contracts in marriage and other intimacies also signals the growing awareness that modern love is not so different from work, if ever it was. And yet, as marital law is shifting to recognize the changing view of marriage, the same pulls and conflicts between sharing and separating, between individual autonomy and merging, between love and the marketplace, continue to plague those who search for the perfect legal instrument.

11

———•———

Investing in Children

Many parents would say they never thought of their children
as investments—they just had them. But in the final analysis,
children are investments, calculated or not. Indeed, children represent the largest investment that most married couples make,
considering the time, money, and involvement they require which
might have gone to something else. Most married people make
this investment, because they expect the benefits will far outweigh
the costs. And today, the main benefit they expect to reap is love,
love so deep and unique that it is considered priceless, and irre-
placeable, worth any cost.

Just a few generations ago, the investment that children repre-
sented was profoundly different. Until the late nineteenth century, Americans had children out of financial need. Those who
lived on farms needed help to do the work, and in cities, poor
parents counted on their children's wages. Not so long ago, having
children was also the system of social security: parents could count
on their children to care for them when they got to be old.

Today, parents only joke about such an idea. "My children will
take care of me when I'm old," they laugh, because they know how
unlikely this is. In fact, many parents worry that they'll still be
supporting their children in their own old age. This profound
change in what we put into children and what we can expect to get
from them has taken place in just a few generations.

The transformation of the American child from an economic
asset to an economically worthless but emotionally priceless object
occurred within the sixty-year period from about 1870 to 1930,
according to a persuasive study by sociologist Viviana Zelizer.[1]

She has documented this transformation by describing the dramatic changes in child labor laws and practices, mourning conventions for dead children, and child adoption patterns during these years. The changes in the use of children as workers was achieved after considerable social and political conflict, and it was associated with shifting economic needs. In the nineteenth century, American industries required unskilled workers, and children were a cheap source of labor. But by the early twentieth century, the influx of immigrants provided a new source of cheap labor, and industry began to need more skilled and educated workers. As children were no longer needed in factories, middle-class reformers began to define child labor as a moral problem, and they created a political movement resulting in compulsory education and restrictive labor laws.

It took longer for this movement to affect children living and working on family farms, where work was seen as more wholesome, and where the need for cheap labor had not yet been reduced by immigration or mechanization. But, eventually, the movement against child labor spread from the urban middle class to the urban poor and finally to the farms. According to Zelizer, by the late 1930s it was considered exploitative to make children work for wages or for more than a few hours at home, and working-class children, like middle-class children, were increasingly valued for their emotional return rather than for their economic contribution. Today, child "work" for wages is unusual and work for children is generally justified only to the extent that it can be viewed as "educational" or character building.

Zelizer argues that the emergence of children as objects of love during this period was also revealed by radically different responses to child deaths. Until the nineteenth century, the death of a young child or an infant was not considered a great tragedy. Often children were buried in unmarked places in the backyard, much as a pet might be today. But in the nineteenth century, Americans began to have elaborate funerals for children and to go into deep mourning when a child died; the death of a child was now viewed as an inconsolable loss because so much love had been invested.

Social historians have speculated on the reasons why children gained such high sentimental value in the nineteenth century. According to some demographic theories, the falling birth and

mortality rates in the nineteenth century increased the value of
each child. As this argument went, as long as death claimed so
many young children, parents remained emotionally aloof because it would have been unwise for them to get too attached to
such "ephemeral" beings. Once they were more likely to live, and
once parents had fewer of them, the emotional value of each one
increased.

Other historians reject this argument, and claim that the shift
toward regarding a child's death as a tragedy actually preceded
the drop in mortality rates. In any case, the sentimentalization of
children was clearly part of a broader shift toward sentimentaliz-
ing the family more generally, and increasingly seeing the family
as a haven for love and intimacy.

Zelizer also points to changes in the baby market as the value of
a child shifted from money to love. Healthy, Caucasian babies are
scarce and valuable objects these days, and specialty services and
lawyers have begun to act as brokers for acquiring them. While
the courts are still undecided about the question of surrogate-
mother contracts, it is clear that today many would pay a lot for a
healthy, Caucasian baby. In contrast, Zelizer reports that in the
nineteenth century an unwed mother had to pay a "baby farm" to
take an infant off her hands. A baby, having little economic value,
was considered a worthless liability, and most died in these farms
after the fee from the mother had been collected. In contrast,
orphaned boys who were old enough to work were attractive
enough to fetch a price in so-called foster homes. Today, the
situation is reversed. Older children are not so attractive to parents who want to adopt because they are viewed as too risky and
problematic as love objects. On the other hand, people are willing
to pay a fortune for the right kind of baby, because a baby is a
perfect sentimental object—easy to love, and still unformed
enough to mold into what one wants.

One reason why children have become so important as a source
of love is that, increasingly, they are the only permanent love
relations people have in this society. Geographic mobility has sev-
ered ties with siblings and parents, and with half the marriages
ending in divorce, people are much more likely to have a permanent relationship with their children than with a spouse. Here,
one thinks especially of women, who are less likely than men to
remarry. But men who recouple after divorce may also rely on

their children for enduring love. I think of one twice-divorced man I know who came to this conclusion: "If you want to have a lasting relationship, have children. When I look at my children, I have a tie I've never had with anyone else. With children, you don't get that high, intense rush you have at the beginning of romance, but for constancy of intimacy, nothing replaces children."

Oddly, children are filling in where spouses are taking off. For many divorced mothers who don't remarry, children are their main day-to-day companions. And for some divorced men who don't want to remarry, children provide reassuring confirmation of their identities as heterosexual and emotionally mature men. With the back-up of children, they can avoid having to get married again, and still maintain a respectable image. The love for children is not entirely unselfish: they fill emotional needs if not financial ones. Aside from wanting to secure a love that is permanent, many parents have children to make up for the regrets of their own early years. They want to raise children as they would like to have been raised, and so give themselves another chance.

Some people find in their love for children a glimmer of immortality and a cushion against death. The sadness of losing parents and other loved ones and of aging oneself has always been muted a little by the thought that room must be made for the next generation. In the Jewish mourner's prayer there is a moving passage consoling those who grieve with the reminder that older people must die so that the young may live. But some are more comforted by the idea that their children will give them immortality by carrying their own genes or values into the future after they are gone.

One man I spoke with, an extremely gifted and successful developer and architect, told me his fantasy that his two sons, in unison, would carry his work and values into the future. At the age of fifty he had accumulated about $30 million, and was trying to figure out how to structure his will. He thought it wrong to leave a fortune that size to his sons unless he could be sure they would put it to some worthwhile use. If they were just going to spend it without doing something socially useful, he preferred to give them enough to be comfortable and to leave the rest to a foundation. But his real hope was that his sons would join forces to carry on what he had started. He'd been successful both as a creative architect and as a partner in an innovative development firm. One son, he believed, would make a good architect, while the other had good business sense. I listened as he shared this scheme with his nineteen-year-old son, telling him that with his brother he could carry his father's torches into the future. I was impressed with his son's sensible reply. After the boy listened for a long time he gently answered, "I wouldn't think of it as carrying your torches, but as a partnership with David."

Still, the father would not be deterred, and recalled his own childhood in a wealthy and prominent midwestern family. When his family went into town, everyone knew who they were, and at church, there were two pews that belonged to the extended family. Now, living on the west coast as a bachelor and part-time father since his divorce ten years before, he missed belonging to a "dynasty" (or, perhaps, to a family) and liked to think his sons would form a new dynasty built around his legacy.

The primacy of love for children has become taken so much for granted that we are stunned by the occasions that violate this principle. Recently, newspapers across the nation carried the story of an eleven-year-old boy who was being "dumped" by his middle-class parents who had adopted him along with a biological brother six years before: "Complaining that they had failed to 'bond' with their eleven-year-old adopted son, a suburban Chicago couple left the boy with an orphanage, then went to court to sever ties with the child."[2] According to reports, the boy made a tape recording for his parents, pleading to be allowed to come home, but they refused to listen to it. His public guardian was suing for the boy's right to have weekly visits with his brother, and on the child's behalf, another suit was filed against the parents seeking damages for emotional distress.

After the case was publicized, several families called the adoption agency, offering to take the boy, but state agencies were really shocked when they also heard from other adoptive parents who called to ask whether they, too, could give back their children. According to the report, 13 percent of all adopted children were returned to state officials last year, and among children who are considered "difficult" placements because of older age or physical or emotional problems, the percentage of "disrupted" adoptions runs about 25 percent. Commenting on the story, experts blamed the unrealistic expectations adoptive parents often have, thinking they are acquiring a family that matches the television situation comedies: "This is not like going to the 5-and-10-cent store, where you can return something if you decide you don't like it."[3]

Stories like this shock us because we've made a secular religion out of love for children. The failure to bond with a child or the wish to return a child one no longer wants are unimaginable. Yet part of the shock also comes from seeing, in these stories, a disturbingly common reality about parents and children: sometimes parents simply don't love their children and wish to end the relationship, and vice versa. It's well known that the majority of divorced fathers fail to pay child support. Once out of daily contact, it's apparently common for many to withdraw emotionally, and once uninvolved, they resent having to pay. As one man tried to explain to me, the process of becoming alienated from your child after you divorce is no more mysterious than the process of becoming disengaged from a former spouse: you forget about them when you become involved with a new partner and new children.

Now that we have no-fault divorce from spouses, and accept the right of any individual to dissolve a marriage they no longer want, is it possible that we could extend the principle to ties with parents and children? It's hard to imagine, but in some ways it's the logical extension of the values we bring to marriage law. Within one recent month, the Phil Donahue television show devoted one program to children who wish to formally divorce their parents, and another to parents who threw their adult children out of the house.

A man I know told me recently that his father disappeared when he was five and he lived alone with his mother until sixteen. At that point, her unpleasant boyfriend moved in, and he decided to move out. He had established a warm friendship with an older couple, who shared his interest in ice-skating, and asked whether he might live with them. They agreed, and at sixteen he moved. Some years later, he legally changed his name to theirs, since they seemed more like parents to him than his biological mother. He felt no guilt at "divorcing" her since she had abandoned him first by letting an abusive man move in, and he had a great deal more in common with the parents he chose. Yet many years later, when his biological father turned up in the city where he lived—he had come to spend the last six months of his life alone at a VA hospital, dying of cancer—the son felt an obligation to visit this man once a week, though he was a virtual stranger. That is the paradox of family life: sometimes we have nothing in common with parents or siblings, other than blood. At times we can accept this and leave them behind; at other times we are bound by guilt.

The idea of divorcing one's parents is really not so incomprehensible, given the fragility of modern family life and the basic orientation of our legal system. Above all, our laws protect the rights and freedoms of the individual over and above the principle of obligation or responsibility for one another. We certainly have no obligations to siblings—as several recent news reports on controversial medical dilemmas have implied. One was the story of a middle-aged woman who conceived and gave birth to a baby in hopes the infant could provide bone marrow for her teenage daughter who was dying of leukemia. Many people were shocked that a baby might be used this way, to keep a sibling alive. Another story told of an estranged father who was suing to force his three-year-old twins to be tested for bone-marrow compatibility with his older son who would also die without a closely related donor. The twins' mother had taken the position that her children should not be forced to assume any risk, no matter how small, in a medical procedure, since they were healthy. The father's suit was quickly dismissed. Although in both cases these were not siblings who knew each other or could exercise any real choice to take the risk or make the sacrifice, the stories pose interesting questions about where responsibility begins and ends within the family. What would we make of adults who refused to give their blood or marrow to a parent or child or sibling with whom they'd shared a lifetime and a home? The law would be on their side.

Certainly our laws, even if they're not well enforced, hold parents responsible for financially supporting their children. At the same time, there's a common sentiment that we owe a responsibility toward children not only on an individual basis but on a social one. It's generally believed that one has children partly to make a contribution to society. I don't know if that's why anyone actually has children, but once they do, many people claim this as a virtue of parenthood. Maybe that's why there's such a gulf between people who have children and people who don't. They're not just divided by the contrast in their life-styles and interests. When people don't want to have children, they're commonly viewed (by those who do) as socially deficient: selfish, immature, or undeveloped.

It's no wonder that parents resent the freedom of those who choose to be childless. Just a few years ago, some economists calculated that a middle-class family was likely to spend about $100,000 raising each child until the age of eighteen. Now, that figure sounds ridiculously low. As in marital relations, most parents don't start counting the bills out loud until they feel hurt and unloved by their children. It's when teenagers start using the house as a hotel, a place to sleep and eat, that parents start to add up the numbers.

Of course, many teenagers do treat their parents as checkbooks. And, many parents wind up bribing their children for love when love is not otherwise forthcoming. Observant grandparents know that once the grandchildren are over the age of six, they'd better arrive bearing gifts if they want to ensure a warm welcome.

Recalling how easy it was for their own parents to control them through guilt, many of my friends are shocked by the brazen and unembarrassed selfishness of their children. One of my friends will always recall his son's teenage and young adult years with an image of the youth obliviously tanning himself on a chaise lounge in the backyard, cordless phone in pocket, while his father staggered around him pushing a heavy lawnmower. A mother I know who works a double shift to send her daughter to an expensive college couldn't understand why the girl was stockpiling huge quantities of shampoo and other supplies while she was living at home during the summer. When she saw her daughter packing cartons of these items to be shipped to school via United Parcel Service, she asked if they didn't sell shampoo in Boston. To her shock, her daughter patiently explained that she had bought a year's supply of everything she needed while living at home, because these purchases were charged to her mother's grocery bill and wouldn't have to come out of her allowance.

Another mother I know complains that she "can't say anything" to her two grown daughters. If she makes any demands or expresses her deepest feelings, she's likely to lose all contact with them. How different is this from the abused wife who accepts any terms in her marriage because she couldn't stand to lose her husband? Teresa Cuneo, the lottery winner, may have been exceptionally injured by her children's selfishness, but her sentiments are not that uncommon. Many older mothers told me, "We cared for our children, but they don't care for us." If the presidents of the United States can't count on their children not to embarrass them, who can? The reciprocal obligation and responsibility between generations that once seemed so unproblematic has unraveled in modern times.

The costs of raising children are also much more daunting than they used to be. I was struck by this last week while visiting my talented childhood friend Jill. She is now an attorney, and her husband is a physician. My friends are relieved that their children have earned high enough grades to be admitted to a prestigious state university, because despite their two professional incomes, they couldn't have afforded to send them to comparable private colleges. I was remembering that Jill's parents, poor European refugees who spoke broken English and earned practically nothing, had somehow saved enough money to send Jill to an Ivy League college.

This isn't an isolated example. The shocking cost of sending a child to private college and the fact that so many parents do is perhaps the most convincing evidence of how hard parents still work for their children. Yet it's become even less affordable than it was for an earlier, poorer generation for other reasons, too. Jill's parents saved enough out of their meager wages to send their daughter to an expensive school because their daughter and her future had always been their entire life. Today, parents like Jill and her husband have become accustomed to a comfortable lifestyle, and they're not about to live like paupers to send their children to college. One more often sees that kind of all-out sacrifice and exclusive focus on the children from parents who have never lived well. Today, I see it most dramatically in families that have immigrated from Asian countries, where parents somehow manage to make valedictorians out of their children even though they can barely speak English themselves.

There is also the question of what kind of control money can provide for parents. In my youth, parental control was rarely challenged openly, even if it was surreptitiously evaded. Today, many parents are resigned to being unable to control their children. All they have in the way of influence is the use of money. A middle-class mother I know told her daughter, who was not interested in college, that she would give her a car as long as she stayed in college and maintained a B average. If her daughter didn't want to go to school, she could get a low-paying job and support herself, but in that case, she'd get nothing from her parents. The mother also presented her daughter with a sample budget to drive home the point that with the salary she'd command as a high-school graduate, she'd be looking at a lifetime of living in studio apartments and taking the bus. Where parents are disappointed by their children's values, there is always the chance that money can provide leverage.

On the other hand, parents who shell out huge sums of money are often shocked to learn that money still doesn't guarantee control, or even the usual rights of consumers. One mother I know who paid a fortune for her son's college education was shocked to discover that he'd flunked out in his third year. Although she'd been paying the bills, she never received any warning from the school that he was in academic trouble, and her son had certainly not kept her informed. When she called the school to ask why no one had told her what was going on, she learned that while she was entitled to pay for her son's tuition, she was not entitled to any information about her son or his record at school. Since the early 1970s college students over the age of eighteen have been guaranteed the right to privacy, even from their parents who pay the bills.

The success or failure of children is also a sensitive point in the experience of children as an investment. Because parents pour so much into their children, it's almost impossible for them not to think of their children as extensions or symbols of themselves. Children who are bright, successful, and attractive reflect well on their parents; the child who fails is an embarrassment. And so, it often happens that children become the ultimate status symbols for their parents, enhancing or detracting the image they present to the world.

Since parents do invest so much in their children, even our legal system is confused about the economic value of children and the question of whether children can be bought and sold. Not long ago, these issues came to public attention when the courts had to decide the fate of "Baby M"—did she belong to her birth mother or the parents who had contracted for her conception and birth? Were contracts arranging for surrogate births even legal? While questions of surrogacy contracts have still not been resolved, it's clear that a gray market has developed for Caucasian babies, since they are scarce and much in demand.

Parents who want such a baby even have to market themselves. A woman I know who's in the market for an infant described how she and her husband had "registered" at a number of private agencies offering "identified" adoption. These agencies introduce would-be parents to prospective mothers and facilitate the transfer. In the first step of the process, the couple writes an autobiography that gets published in a booklet, much like a weekly real estate listing, which expectant mothers are given to read. The mothers-to-be (mainly teenagers) read through the listings and select the homes that interest them, and a meeting is arranged. The couple I know was advised by their lawyer that they could market themselves best by writing an autobiography that would appeal to the mind of a pregnant teenager—they should appear like the parents she would have wanted for herself.

The "identified" plan offers advantages all around. The mother gets to exercise choice over where her baby will be placed, while the couple gets to meet the mother—thereby gaining a chance to judge or question her about the genetic background (and, therefore, the value) of the child. As my friend observed, obtaining a baby these days is like purchasing a work of art.

The idea of treating a baby as a commodity is still offensive enough to most people that there is great sensitivity around the issue, and legal efforts not to let the market operate without regulation. Many of the same contradictions apply to parents who sue over the wrongful death of a child. As Viviana Zelizer pointed out in her history of the "priceless child," there is much uneasiness about commercializing the value of a child. As a consequence, many states retain statutes that limit monetary awards for the wrongful death of a child to pecuniary losses—that is, compensation for the loss of the child's economic contribution. Strictly speaking, parents are not supposed to be compensated for pain and anguish when a child dies because of the wrongful action of another, but awards indicate that most states have extended the notion of pecuniary loss to include "companionship" of the child and, therefore, the whole range of parental feelings. After all, as Zelizer argues, if the courts took a strict interpretation of pecuniary loss, lawyers would be placed in the absurd position of having to calculate the lost monetary value of a child's paper route or lemonade stand. In fact, awards to bereaved parents occasionally exceed a million dollars, because the loss of love is perceived to be so great.[4]

The factor of gender also complicates the kind of investment that children represent. Until recently, a woman's capital has been her love. While the economically useful child of a hundred and fifty years ago was "owned" by the father, the emotionally priceless child of today is considered the mother's special asset. That is why mothers are the star witnesses in suits over a child's death. Zelizer quotes a psychiatrist who testified in a wrongful death trial that "A mother really invests a lot of herself into her children. . . . It is like investing in Blue Chip Stocks. . . . This is what a mother is going to give to society. . . . If anything happens to that child . . . you lose your investment. That is why [mothers] have this prolonged neurotic reaction and long grief . . . after such a loss."[5]

It seems that individuals, like the courts, are currently confused about the question of children as investments. While the courts struggle with questions of surrogacy contracts and value, most individuals struggle with uncertainty and lack of guidance about what parents and children owe each other, and where the obligation ends. The contradictions are staggering because at a time when children have been sentimentalized as the most enduring and important love objects, we also commonly witness evidence of the failures of that love—the millions of children who are emotionally and financially abandoned by their fathers, the millions of parents who feel exploited by their children. The contradictions are also evident in the societal response to investing in children. Parents sentimentalize children and also invest in them a huge share of their emotional and financial resources. Our culture collectively sentimentalizes children, too, but as a society we invest relatively little in the next generation. On every measure of public support for children, from maternity leaves to education and school lunches and tax benefits, we collectively invest much less in children than most of the industrialized nations of the world.

It's hard to pick up a newspaper without seeing yet another report on the dismal condition of our educational system, and the fact that American children have much lower levels of educational achievement than their peers in the industrialized nations of Asia and Europe. Reading this, people shake their heads at one more sign of the decline of the United States. And yet it seems the country has stopped thinking about the future and providing for it. Unlike our parents, who earned much less, those of us who are baby-boomers find it very difficult to save. On the public level, the nation can't seem to deal with the national debt, and on the individual level, many of us can't get through the month without charging even more to our credit cards. The inability to curtail consumption and provide for the future is both personal and social.

Many theories have been offered for why we can't seem to save or invest in the future, either as individuals, or as a nation. One popular, though dubious, explanation is that we can't save because we think the end is near, that the threat of nuclear war has created a generation that can only live in the present because it doesn't have faith in any future.

It used to be common to link "present" and "future" orientations to stereotypes of social classes. In popular culture and in social science, the middle class has been traditionally portrayed as future-oriented: geared toward planning, expecting improvement, and able to defer immediate gratification in order to reach long-term goals. In contrast, the poor have always been portrayed as present-oriented: addicted to immediate gratification and unable to sacrifice or plan for the future. Suddenly, the middle-class is not looking so future-oriented. The reason may be that future-orientation is not intrinsically related to any particular class, but rather to a confidence in the future that used to be more solid in the middle class.

Anthropologist Eliot Liebow made this argument in his classic study of a group of unemployed black men who hung out on a Washington, D.C., street corner during the early 1960s. Liebow observed that, indeed, they lived as though there might not be any tomorrow, but argued why that orientation was not a product of their class or culture but rather their realistic assessment of their situation. Time orientation, he pointed out, is not a function of class but of prospects for the future:

> Whenever people of whatever class have been uncertain,
> skeptical or downright pessimistic about the future, "I want
> mine right now" has been one of the characteristic re-
> sponses. . . . In wartime, especially, all classes tend to
> slough off conventional restraints on sexual and other be-

havior (i.e., become less able or less willing to defer gratification). And when inflation threatens, darkening the fiscal future, persons who formerly husbanded their resources with commendable restraint almost stampede one another rushing to spend their money. Similarly, it seems that future-time orientation tends to collapse toward the present when persons are in pain or under stress.[6]

One common explanation of why baby-boomers can't save is consistent with this idea about dim prospects for the future. It's often argued that the general decline of the nation, the deterioration of the planet, and growing up in the shadow of the cold war, have made us reluctant to sacrifice for an uncertain future. While this is undoubtedly true, there are other, more material, factors that are equally, if not more, important.

During the last few years, we've had a respite from inflation, but the heavy and sustained inflation of the late 1970s and early 80s seems to have left a permanent mark on this generation, as an earlier generation was marked by the depression. Emotionally, it seems we expect inflation. It's always a surprise to hear that prices haven't risen very much, and we keep spending as if to keep ahead of the erosion of the dollar. But more important than expectations is the real decline in the standard of living that so many have experienced. In the last twenty years, between the early 1970s and the present, it's a fact that inflation-adjusted income was hardly increased for a large segment of the population, and in many cases the standard of living and real buying power (such as the ability to buy a house) have dramatically diminished. Even middle-class people have to work harder, spend more, and save less in order to maintain the life-style they had twenty years ago. Today, few can afford to buy a house or have children without two incomes and enormous loans. On the individual level, the failure to save is less a matter of pessimism about the future than economic necessity.

At the social level, if public policy is any measure, there seems to be more choice in the decision not to provide for the future, and specifically, not to invest in the next generation. It seems we've accepted the condition of widespread child poverty—the fact that over twenty percent of American children and almost half of black and hispanic children live in poverty-stricken conditions. But as more and more people are recognizing what this will mean for the country as a whole, and not just for the poor, there is a growing concern about the consequences of not investing in our children.

While the deterioration of child welfare has long been a concern of liberal politics, some have argued that business interests are starting to become alarmed too. One observer, Jonathan Rauch[7] claims that business leaders are increasingly concerned about the shrinking supply of educated, qualified young workers. And, because baby-boomers are having fewer children, and a much larger portion of American children are growing up in poverty, there is increasing concern not only about the shortage of qualified workers but also the ability of the next generation to support the retirement and old age of the large baby-boom generation in just about twenty years from now. There is legitimate fear that with increased longevity and the explosion of health care costs, our social security system will collapse under the weight of the boom generation and the limitations of its offspring.

As Rauch argues, there are many reasons for the decline in fertility and the impoverishment of today's children, but our policies for distributing wealth are a major part of the problem. The United States is practically alone among industrialized nations in lacking financial benefits to parents for childrearing or paid work leave for parents. Rauch asked various experts why Europeans are so much more generous than Americans with public benefits for families with children, and was told that it partly stems from different conceptions about children as "capital." They answer that in Europe, children are viewed as crucial resources, and parents are viewed as making a contribution to society by producing the future labor force that will finance the social security system. In the United States, families have been putting more and more effort into raising children. Sustaining a middle-class life-style with children requires two incomes and a double shift for mothers who usually do most of the housework after coming home from the workplace. Yet our public policies don't acknowledge their efforts or their contribution, or the fact that the impoverishment of today's children will have consequences for everyone in the country. In addition, many parents today are also caring for aging parents since the society makes little provision for their care, and, again, the burden falls primarily on women.

According to Rauch, there may be a new convergence of political interests around the necessity of supporting children. Liberals and social activists may have a new ally in the corporate world. According to Frank Levy, one of Rauch's informants: "In the seventies, corporations had workers coming out of their ears, so they didn't have to worry about the quality of the work force. They could just discard what they couldn't use. But once you have the labor force growing slowly and you start bumping into scarcity, then you have to assess the quality of the whole work force, because you can't just throw away the bottom quarter or twenty percent. Then you realize that we're all in this together."[8]

There are still profound differences between the right and the left about what to do. Liberals want business-supported parental leave and government-supported day care, while conservatives want to encourage mothers to stay home and raise larger families with the assistance of tax incentives. Perhaps when child-care reaches the crisis it's headed for we'll see some new alliances, as Rauch suggests, in favor of committing public resources to an investment in children.

Parents were once willing to sacrifice everything for their children, confident that their children would support them in old age. Today, parents continue to sacrifice, but no longer count on their children to see them through a long retirement that contains endless possibilities for catastrophically expensive illnesses and medical treatments, ranging from Alzheimer's disease to total hip replacements. Families were once able to govern the exchange between generations and provide for their mutual support, but this system has broken down with inflation, divorce, geographic mobility, the baby boom, and the baby bust. The responsibility for investing in children may finally have to be assumed by the public.

12

—•—

Squaring the Family Circle

The trend toward freeing individuals from the control of the family has become apparent not only in popular culture, but in the law. Laws reflect the values of a culture, and also serve to encourage or undermine those values. The laws governing family life, and especially the marital relationship, have been changing dramatically in the past two decades.

Until recently, there was broad agreement that marriage meant the merging of individuals into a social and legal unit. Marriage was viewed as permanent and monogamous, and there was an assumption that partners were linking their life fates with each other. In recent times, the entire draft of the law, as the drift of society, has gone in the direction of seeing spouses as more separated individuals, capable of having conflicting interests and of having an existence outside the unit.

Until the last century, the marital couple was seen as a single unit legally controlled by the husband. By the end of the nineteenth century, the legal doctrine of "coverture" (whereby the wife's interests are suspended and incorporated into those of her husband) was beginning to erode. New laws gave married women the right to buy, own, and sell property, and to make contracts. But until roughly two decades ago, married people were still commonly viewed as forming a merged entity, and this assumption is still reflected in special laws for joint taxes, property, and inheritance.

Recently, the drift of the law has been toward treating spouses more as individuals. For example, laws now allow husbands and wives to sue each other. The most dramatic instance of the trend toward greater separation has been the movement toward no-fault divorce, which is based on the assumption that no one should have to stay in an unhappy marriage, because individual happiness is the primary goal of marriage. That shift in the law acknowledges a new belief that the family exists for the individual rather than vice versa, according to legal scholar Marjorie Shultz.[1]

Until two decades ago, divorce was granted only on the basis of "marital fault," such as adultery, mental cruelty, and desertion, and only with the consent of the "innocent" party. Today, divorce is generally granted whenever either party claims that the marriage has "broken down." As Lenore Weitzman demonstrated in her study of the "divorce revolution," the reforms of the 1970s have often been devastating for women.[2]

Prior to no-fault divorce, an "innocent" wife had a financial bargaining advantage over a husband who wanted a divorce, since he needed her consent. Fault on his part was also a factor in the financial settlements that courts would prescribe. Today, no-fault divorce assumes that both partners are capable of supporting themselves, and that a person is entitled to support from a former spouse only in cases of dire need—and even then, only a small amount for a short "transitional" period. While alimony was once considered to be owed by a partner who had committed marital misconduct, contemporary "maintenance" awards are extremely small and short-term. In her analysis, Weitzman describes how even long-term homemakers in their fifties and sixties were typically given only two or three years of modest payments to "rehabilitate" themselves so they could presumably become self-supporting. More recently, the injustice of that practice has caused the courts to make longer support awards.

The other major change in marital property and divorce law has been the shift toward "equitable distribution" whereby all property acquired during marriage (other than inheritances) is considered the property of both spouses and subject to division upon divorce, regardless of who earned it. This principle operates in all states with equitable distribution except for those cases where partners have entered into a properly executed legal contract (an antenuptial or nuptial agreement) that specifies a different division of resources in the event of divorce. States vary according to what is considered marital property (e.g., the value of a professional degree, earning capacity, expected future income) and what is considered an "equitable" division. California is one of only eight states that requires judges to divide marital property equally between the spouses. Most states give the court discretion in dividing property, and studies indicate that, on average, wives have received about one-third.

As Lenore Weitzman has convincingly argued in her extensive study of the divorce laws and their impact, this figure overstates the real proportion of property that goes to the wife. This is because for most families, the real wealth lies not in savings or literal assets but in the investment in the career and earning capacities of the spouses, especially the husband. As Weitzman points out, in less than a year the average couple can earn more than all the tangible assets they have acquired. But this real wealth is generally not included in the legal definition of marital property. Furthermore, courts tend to undervalue even what they consider marital property because it's easy for people to disguise the value of their businesses or assets, and wives typically don't have enough money to pay for expensive search and discovery procedures.[3]

As a result, it's by now a well-known fact that divorce has very different economic consequences for men and women. There is a myth that everyone suffers financially after a divorce. However, most studies demonstrate that while women and children suffer enormous financial losses, most men actually come out ahead after the initial two years. Reviewing all the data, Weitzman found that at all levels of income, women were much poorer than men after divorce, and that children and wives of upper-middle-class families experienced the greatest relative deprivation after divorce. Even the argument that most of the men would need most of their money because they would soon be supporting another family was not supported by the evidence. Surveys indicate that men tend to remarry women who have higher incomes than their first wives, and support their new families at a level well above the one enjoyed by their former wives and children.[4]

In their study of the psychological impact of divorce on families in affluent Marin County, California, Judith Wallerstein and Joan Kelly demonstrate that even people who are relatively well-off can be deeply affected by having to sell their house and change their life-style, particularly when the financial loss is not shared equally. In their research, Wallerstein and Kelly found that children frequently compared the financial situations in their mother's and father's households. In divorced families, the postdivorce life-style is not experienced or evaluated in a vacuum. The mother and children frequently compare their standard of living with the way they had lived before. They also compare their current standard of living with that of the husband and his new family.[5] Downward mobility for the wife and children seemed less painful when the father suffered too. When the wife and children lost their former life-style and the father did not, the loss was harder to bear.

One wonders how this experience will affect the next generation and their choices about marriage and careers. Any young woman who takes a hard, objective, look at the consequences of divorce should see that it's risky for her to become financially dependent on a spouse, for she and her children would be in severe jeopardy if she divorced. Under the new laws, women risk more than men if they make the traditional bargain of trading emotional for financial support; their financial dependence will probably outlast their husband's emotional dependence. Contemporary marriages are at least as likely to end in divorce as they are to last, but people tend to take the sentimental view of marriage until they have gone through a divorce.

All forces in our culture—economic, legal, psychological, and ideological—point to the necessity of being autonomous and independent. Yet it's impossible in the context of marriage to act as a free agent. In her discussion of marital law,[6] Susan Prager observes that though our contemporary rhetoric stresses individual responsibility and self-sufficiency, marriage, in fact, is necessarily based on merging—in the sense that people joined in marriage have to make joint decisions, and not necessarily the ones best serving their individual interests. Even when married people are financial equals, they still make decisions that are different from the ones they would make if single. When they make career choices, they have to consider where they will live, what kind of opportunities and stress the choice will create for the other partner, how their choice of work will affect the couple's ability to be together. Married people can't make individualistic decisions, because every choice affects the partner. Prager, therefore, argues that marital property laws should provide for a sharing of marital assets, since marriage is based on sharing.

Other feminists have argued that it's wiser for spouses to maintain separate finances, and that the laws should send a clear and realistic message to women that dependency is not rewarded and will not be rewarded (here, they are talking about spousal support, not child support). In this way, the law, though cold and hard, would eventually foster independence in women. But, as Prager points out, separate property also rewards people for self-interested choices and undermines the possibilities for accommodation that are necessary for long-term unions.

There's evidence that women have been influenced by feminism to prefer separate accounts over pooling money with their spouses as a way of protecting independence in marriage. In their survey[7] of thousands of American couples, Philip Blumstein and Pepper Schwartz discovered that women more oriented to feminist perspectives were less likely to want to pool their money. Research by sociologist Rosanna Hertz indicates that women who do pool their income tend to let their husbands control the finances.[8]

One couple I know took great pains to work out the problem of merging and separation in marriage. It's an issue in every marriage, but these partners have deliberately arranged their finances in the service of preserving individual autonomy and avoiding dependency. They have not negotiated a marriage contract in place of the state laws that would apply if they divorced but have been explicit about their motives for keeping money separate, while recognizing the problems with this choice.

Nancy Foote and David Howell agree that individual autonomy must be primary in their marriage, but they differ on how far to carry the principle. David, especially, is mockingly wistful about the merging that is absent in their marriage. It comes up all the time and is practically a family joke. Once I was riding in a car with them, and as we passed a cemetery, their young children began to question them about the kind of funeral they'd want to have. Both Nancy and David said they'd like to be cremated. "Do you want your ashes mixed together or kept separate?" their seven-year-old daughter asked. "Separate," said Nancy, and David groaned, "Separate in life, separate in death."

Although they've lived together for fourteen years and have

two young children, they have always kept their money entirely separate. They've never had a joint savings or checking account. From their separate funds each pays for personal expenses and precisely half the costs of running the house and taking care of their children. When the phone bill comes, Nancy and David initial and pay for each one's long-distance calls and split the basic monthly fee and taxes, exactly down the middle. Naturally, they've retained their own names, and their children's names are hyphenated.

Taped on their refrigerator, for all the world to see, is a "chit-list" where they record all the money they've spent individually on items to be considered shared expenses: groceries, gasoline for the cars, things for the children. At times, Nancy gets annoyed with David for recording minuscule expenses (fifty cents for a newspaper) she would overlook, or resents paying for long-distance calls to her sister (all calls to her family are treated as her expense) when he's picked up the phone and talked with her sister as long as she has. So, once in a while, she evens things up by adding to the chit list a charge for items that are arguably personal. For example, it's understood that the cost of birth control is a joint expense, while each pays for personal drugstore and grooming items. But annoyed at David's penny splitting, Nancy occasionally sneaks a box of tampons into her grocery bill, rationalizing it on the grounds that tampons could be construed as pertaining to sex and reproduction (a shared category) though she knows that David pays for the equivalent costs of his secondary sexual characteristics—like shaving cream.

Some might ask, what kind of marriage is this, sharing children but not the bills? In fact, it's a pretty good marriage. Anyone who knows this couple can see they genuinely like and respect each other, and unlike many married couples, they're fun to be with, because they speak for themselves and don't force each other into acting as a merged unit.

Their separate finances evolved from circumstance as much as temperament. Their relationship was built in the early seventies, when people in their circles were highly conscious about feminism. But there were other reasons for keeping separate checkbooks. Although they have identical salaries (they are both performing musicians, and each earns about $70,000 a year) David comes from a wealthier family. Half-consciously, keeping separate accounts was a way of recognizing that whatever money he got from his family should not have to be shared.

Mainly, each one brought a fear of dependency into this union. Thinking of her mother, Nancy was afraid of turning into a house-wife and compromising her career once she got married. And David, who is more worried than Nancy about money, didn't want to impose his financial anxieties on his wife.

They're also aware of what has been sacrificed—David wistfully observes that their marriage has the character of friendship and sibling loyalty rather than romance. Although they share their devotion to music as a way of life, they make no pretense of sharing other interests. David is bored by Nancy's passion for feminism, and she doesn't share his involvement with art.

Keeping money separate is also one way they minimize conflict and irritation over different values and habits. Nancy likes to donate her extra money to political and social causes, while David is concerned about saving and investing. He thinks that in a crisis they'd have to depend on his savings, and he doesn't think that's fair. He also considers Nancy wasteful about small purchases, like buying name brand items when she could pay less for generic brands. He prefers to save for big investments, like works of art, and he never buys anything that he couldn't resell for at least what he paid for it.

But even if they quibble over shopping habits, keeping money separate does minimize their larger conflicts. If David were add-ing to his collection of pre-Columbian statues with joint funds, Nancy might be disgusted when she thought about the political causes that were collapsing for lack of money. And when David blew up because Nancy allowed their daughter to bring an expen-sive music box (a gift from David's mother) to school, where it was promptly broken, Nancy was able to end the argument by paying to fix it.

In fact, different temperaments and values can be gratifying in a marriage rather than just a source of conflict. Most people look for opposition on some dimensions in their mate. It's liberating to have a partner who's relaxed and unrepressed in ways one is not, but it's easier to enjoy these differences when you don't have to pay for them.

A few years ago, David and Nancy faced a crisis that destroyed the whole edifice of their chit-list economy. Nancy was given a new, long-term contract to perform in the orchestra where they both worked, and David was not. For a while, it looked as though David's performing career was finished. His prospects of getting a position in another good orchestra were very slim, and their chances of getting two positions in the same city were negligible. Because they share child-care, they were not good candidates for a commuter marriage, and since neither wanted to be a teacher, and both loved to perform, their options were limited. In the midst of the crisis, the couple recognized they were financially interdependent. As David put it, they were "merged" until he could be retrained for another career. Nancy's salary and his savings and inheritance would have to be considered common property.

At first, David showed an interest in staying home and developing his interest in painting. But Nancy considered this impractical and unseemly and worried that without a job her husband would lose his self-esteem and slip into a funk. In a crisis, it was all right to pool funds, but she never wanted either one to be financially dependent on the other.

As it turned out, David's job was saved a few months later when the orchestra had a change in management and, reversing its decision, gave him a long-term contract. With his job secure, the chit-list system was reinstated. But looking back at the crisis, they are wistful of that time of greater sharing and the breakdown of their self-sufficiency. Both thought it was one of the closest times in their marriage, though Nancy doubts that what felt good in a crisis would have worked in the long run. "He's overtly more dissatisfied with the chit list and with the children's hyphenated names and says it's like a corporation, not a family. But I need autonomy and we need to be able to spend money in different ways."

Speaking of the ideology that would have us believe the family should be the sanctuary from the marketplace, Nancy endorses the principle of sharing in the family, but can't blind herself to its effect on women:

> The comforts of the family have been provided by
> women—women giving and not getting. The family meets
> infantile needs. The woman can be dependent, and the
> man can get personalized services surrounded by the ideol-

ogy of love—he can believe his wife washes his dirty clothes out of love, and he doesn't have to acknowledge that this person is his butler and that he pays his butler a wage. David and I both have yearnings for the family to be different from the marketplace, but the family has always been an economic institution. One of the contradictions of feminism and chit lists is that it makes the calculating, market mentality more explicit, although feminism would otherwise favor sharing and collective values. The contradiction is that the family is supposed to be a place of loving and altruism, and here we are, running it like a market, tit for tat. But we are trained for the marketplace, and financial independence provides symbolic and material props for autonomy. Money gives you options.

They divide child-care and house chores as precisely as they divide money, being among the 5 percent of American couples that even try for equality. Here again, Nancy is aware of the contradictions. You can break down the work that must be done into quantifiable measures of time, but the partners will still have different perceptions of what they've done, and some work can't really be divided. And, always, there is the underlying dissatisfaction with the bookkeeping attitude. "You can divide the time spent on child care, cooking, doing dishes, but the more you work out those things the more you think it's like a factory—punching in and punching out. Especially when it concerns doing things for the children, where you enjoy it and it's a voluntary pleasure."

At the time they bought their house, David had more cash and put in a larger share of the down payment. To pay him back, and to give herself equity in the house, Nancy took an extra job teaching at a summer music camp, even though she was in the last stages of pregnancy. One of her feminist friends, seeing Nancy, eight months pregnant, dragging herself to work in ninety-five degree weather when she might have been on vacation, was horrified and said so. "What is this? You're a family. You're working to pay your husband?"

Indeed, the limits (and sibling-like rivalry) of trying to keep things exactly even are evident in their behavior. While Nancy was in labor delivering their first child, David, distressed at seeing his wife suffering the pain of natural childbirth, whispered to her while she sweated and panted that this would make up for the gardening she didn't do. Looking back at it, Nancy generously forgives the remark, though she's not convinced she owed David anything because he took care of the yard. After all, she asks, "Is gardening really a household chore, or should it count as a hobby and personal pleasure?"

Nancy and David may be more explicit and aware of the ways that they count and measure, but counting and measuring are a part of any relationship—whether its acknowledged or not. So is the reality of separate and sometimes conflicting interests. Whether couples pool money or keep it separate, the real problem families face is how to have the pleasure and security of sharing and joining together as a unit while making room for the strong individualism and autonomy that are so basic to this culture. People express these conflicts with money, and try to solve them with money, just as they use money to deal with every other emotion that comes up in relationships: love, anger, loss, jealousy, and fear.

One thing I like about the way that David and Nancy deal with money is that they're facing the complex realities of family life and making choices about what kind of relationship they want to have. The ways they manage money are directed at achieving the things that are important to them: equality, independence, and the pleasures of their interests, both separate and joined. Of course, this also can be done when partners pool their money, but when assets are pooled it's a little easier for the more dominating member of the relationship to control things while the couple pretends it isn't happening.

Pooling can also be a way of covering up unacknowledged conflicts and power imbalances and other problems, but it doesn't make them go away. I think of the woman who put her entire inheritance in joint names with her husband, and allowed him to spend it all on himself, because she didn't want to face the fact that he was using her. I think of the woman who assumed the debts that her husband ran up in restaurants and department stores and with the IRS, because she hated to acknowledge how infantile he was. In her research on dual-career couples, sociologist Rosanna Hertz discovered that when women outearn their husbands and pool their money, they often do it to mask the fact that they earn more.[9] On the last point, it seems that people are growing more comfortable with partnerships in which women outearn men as it becomes more common. However, if the husband's earning less creates dependence or is an expression of dependence, that's a problem, and pooling money to mask the inequality isn't going to improve matters.

Some people, like David, feel that keeping money separate reduces the sense of romance or commitment in a relationship, but there's no reason why independence should be antithetical to romance. Couple relationships model themselves on, or at least incorporate elements of, the sibling bond or the parent-child bond. This makes a certain kind of sense, since these are the formative relationships that shape our identities and expectations in love. I see the sibling relationship as basically an alliance between equals: Though there is always some competition for dominance, the partners are in a roughly equal position. Despite the rivalry, sibling-type partners also see themselves as playmates in a friendly alliance against the outside world. Unlike real siblings, they're not competing for the love of parents, so they can really enjoy the intimacy of "growing up" together.

As philosopher Stanley Cavell has argued,[10] some of the greatest romantic comedies in American film history, the so-called madcap comedies of the thirties and forties such as *The Awful Truth, His Girl Friday, Adam's Rib,* and *The Philadelphia Story,* involved couples who acted like competitive brothers and sisters. Not only were these partners evenly matched in wit and abilities, but also in financial standing or worldly success. In *Adams Rib,* Katherine Hepburn and Spencer Tracy portray a married couple who are fierce rivals in the courtroom. In *His Girl Friday,* Rosalind Russell and Cary Grant spar as reporter and editor as well as romantic partners. They have fun together because they act like mischievous children who make each other laugh. The rivalry within their relationship is not the kind that undermines. In fact, it seems to bring out the best in each, like the pleasure and excitement experienced by competing athletes who admire and like each other; for the same reason, it enhances rather than diminishes the erotic aspects of their relationship. Since the sibling-type relationship is basically one of equals, dependency and guilt are not usually major issues.

People also experience romantic attachments that are unconsciously modeled on the parent-child relationship, which is not an alliance between independent equals but rather a merging between a caretaker and one who needs care. In the parent-child partnership, the emotional gratification comes from the fantasy that one person will provide total care and protection for the other, or rescue and restore the other from earlier hurts or disappointments. Most "serious" fictional love stories involve such rescues and redemptions. They appeal to us emotionally because a part of us always yearns to find someone who will give us whatever a parent failed to give. In real life, the initial gratifying passion and intensity of some love affairs stem from the short-lived but exhilarating belief that the lover will save us.

Because of the power of these emotions, this is the kind of relationship we often think of as "passionate." When we take care of someone or rely on them for care, we do get deeply involved, not only because of the objective dependence, but also because of the transference of feelings we had as children toward our parents. And yet, as many of the people in this book discovered, it is finally not all that gratifying to care for an adult who acts like a child, or to be infantilized as an adult by financial dependence. When people say that being explicit about money or having separate bankbooks ruins the "passion" of relationships, they are often really saying that it dispels the fantasy of recapturing unconditional, parent-child love. But sooner or later, that fantasy is dispelled anyway, since it's unrealistic and unsuitable for anyone but a child. In the long run, people may find greater pleasure in more equal and independent, sibling-type relationships.

The impact of financial independence on commitment between partners is another matter. Being independent makes it easier to get out of a relationship one no longer wants, but on the other hand, financial dependence and merging don't guarantee a stable relationship either. When people have separate finances, it expresses the partners' acknowledgment that they may have separate or different interests, that they may want to make certain choices without asking the other's permission. To some that's a threatening notion, while for others, it's the condition for being able to act like an adult.

The increasing popularity of prenuptial and postnuptial contracts is another expression of the trend toward being more businesslike about marriage, even at the cost of romance. The very rich have always been more likely to have legal contracts before they marry. In recent years, this practice has become more common in the middle class, especially in second marriages, where one or both of the partners has become more cautious after a divorce or feels that their inheritance is owed to their children from a previous marriage.

They are also becoming more popular among people entering marriage for the first time, especially those who bring assets to a marriage, because it's getting harder to avoid the recognition that relationships are not always permanent. Prenuptial contracts that are properly executed give a couple a way to distribute property in case of divorce in a manner different from the rules prescribed by their states. These agreements generally hold up in court, provided that they meet certain conditions, including full disclosure of assets at the time of execution. They are useful in that they provide for a divorce settlement in advance, saving couples the expense of having to go through litigation when they break up. But because these contracts are viewed as unromantic and unfeeling, about half the people who consult lawyers about preparing one decide they can't ask their partner to sign it. An article in the *New York Times* quotes one such person, a successful woman about to marry a man fourteen years her junior: "I actually went so far as to have my lawyer write one up, yet at the last minute I couldn't ask my fiance to sign it. I could not bring up anything that would suggest our marriage might not last forever." According to one frustrated lawyer quoted in the same article, "They don't realize that prenuptial agreements don't kill romance. They just suspend it for a short time."[11]

Prenuptial agreements have also been criticized because of their potential to exploit women, since they are usually demanded by men who have money from women who do not. Typically a woman who signs one is giving up rights to her husband's money that would otherwise be considered hers by state law. But as one writer has noted, "Women are free not to marry men intent on exploiting them: engagements break off over prenuptials."[12]

But are such women really free? Marjorie Shultz, who has written about the legal, social, and philosophical complexities of marriage contracts points out that contract law assumes both parties have entered into the agreement on a level of equality—at least in the sense of their ability to accept or reject the bargain. But when men have most of the power, what kind of fair bargain can possibly be struck?[13] Still, it would seem that in the long run people entering marriage stand to gain more than they lose by being direct, honest, and explicit with each other, and they can wind up with an agreement that's more appropriate for their particular marriage if they devise their own agreement. Losing illusions may be painful in the short run, but it doesn't really change anything beneath the veneer of romance. Unfortunately, people often find the truth too painful to live with, and it could be argued that maintaining relationships may require some illusions. Also, in the final analysis, contracts can't really protect us from the failings of another person. As one lawyer told me, most problems that cause divorce are insoluble, and even though people want to protect themselves with contracts and fix the rules of sex, morality, and love, this can't really be done—because a contract is only as good as the person who signs it.

In the end, we are always left with the truth that while money is power, money doesn't always corrupt feeling so much as it casts a bright light on the underlying issues in family life. Inevitably, these involve ambivalence, conflict, inequality, and competition, as well as love, devotion, and altruism.

Family life is competitive, rife with inequalities, and prone to struggles over control. There is no way the problems can be totally eradicated. Karl Marx predicted that the cash nexus would rid the family of its sentimental veil, and that the obviousness of the monetary relation would liberate people from their illusions and allow them to recognize power and dependency in all institutions. But illusions die hard in love, even when money should make things clear.

A certain amount of conflict and competition will always be present in families. Even close relatives have different values and separate interests, and we yearn for freedom and autonomy as well as safety and connection. When it comes to love, it's hard to avoid competitive feelings, because people tend to be greedy about love, and they don't like to share. At least in our culture, anyone who has ever been around young children must see the passion of these rivalries. Firstborn children usually resent the arrival of a sibling, and younger children feel forever inferior because they are always behind in what they can do. Spouses resent having to share the love and attention of their partner with a child, and they are jealous when a child clearly favors the other partner.

The pain of being displaced by a sibling, or not measuring up to one, is so profound that many people never get over it. That's why they fight over worthless objects when parents die. Others who felt cheated by parents are always looking for other people to support them. It may be love that we want most of all, but we wind up fighting over money. Facing the fact that these rivalries and differences exist may be necessary for dealing with them constructively.

Many people are passive or paralyzed when it comes to dealing with family money, because they feel too guilty or frightened about the realities they will have to face. Recognizing that there is competition and ambivalence, and that people have unequal needs or conflicting ones, doesn't mean that we can't be fair and generous with one another. When we don't make difficult choices about money, we inflict even more damage on those we love. Money is so powerful, and its absence so consequential, that it exerts its own crushing impact. If we choose not to exercise control over money, it winds up controlling our own lives, or the lives we leave behind.

The people I've known who were lucky enough to grow up in loving families usually go on to find some happiness in the loves of their adulthood. For these people, the problems of money are relatively straightforward. They want to use their money to pursue their interests and give things to their children or the people they love; they want to provide for the future and to buy things that give them pleasure. But most of us also bring to relationships the festering wounds of childhood. At some point we were badly hurt or neglected and learned to be careful. Unwittingly we repeat and relive the disappointments we think we've protected ourselves from. Money weaves its way deeply into the texture of the lives we spin, and eventually we can't distinguish ourselves from it. Money represents all things: a measure of our value; a source of power over other people, or a means to be free of them; a way to show care to others and to figure out how much they really care about us.

At the end of her autobiography Kate Simon tells an old Yiddish story to sum up her father's attitude toward his family: "A dying Jewish man is making out his will with the help of a friend.

'But,' the friend protests, 'if you leave the store to your brother Sol, and your house to your sister Rosie, what's left for your wife and children, your family?' 'What family? Rosie, Sol . . . that's my family.' "[14]

It's not simply that money tells the truth about the family, but that most of us have so much of our emotional capital tied up in the accounts of childhood that we are still settling old debts instead of attending to the needs of the present.

Notes

Chapter 1
Love and Money

1. Paul Glastris et al., "Baby Boomers Hit the Inheritance Jackpot," *U.S. News & World Report*, May 7, 1990, 27. Also see Nick Ravo, "A Windfall Nears in Inheritances from the Richest Generation, *New York Times*, July 22, 1990, E4.
2. Ravo, E4.
3. Francine Russo, "Live-in Divorce: Tortured Couples Who Have to Stay Together," *New York* 23, 5, February 5, 1990, 40–46.
4. Kenneth Boulding, *A Preface to Grants Economics: The Economy of Love and Fear* (New York: Praeger, 1981), 25.
5. Boulding, 25.
6. Lionel Trilling, *The Liberal Imagination* (New York: Doubleday, 1953), 258.
7. Viviana Zelizer, "The Social Meaning of Money: Special Monies," *American Journal of Sociology* 95 (1989): 342–377. Also Viviana Zelizer, "Special Monies: Gift Monies," paper presented to American Sociological Association, August 1989.

Chapter 2
Rude Awakenings

1. Kate Simon, *Bronx Primitive: Portraits in a Childhood* (New York: Viking, 1982), 47.
2. Arlie Hochschild, *The Managed Heart* (Berkeley: University of California Press, 1983) 166.
3. Maureen Orth, "What's Love Got To Do With It?," *Vanity Fair* 53, August 1990, 128.

Chapter 3
Not Enough to Go Around

1. Daniel Goleman, "For Each Sibling, There Appears to be a Different Family," *New York Times*, July 26, 1987, C13.
2. Adrienne Rich, "Split At The Root," in *Fathers: Reflections by Daughters*, ed. Ursula Owen (New York: Pantheon, 1983).
3. Arthur Miller, "The Price," in *The Portable Arthur Miller* (New York: Viking, 1971), 371.

Chapter 4
The Cash Nexus

1. Georg Simmel, *The Philosophy of Money*, Trans. Tom Bottomore and David Frisby (London: Routledge and Kegan Paul, 1978).
2. E. M. Forster, *Howard's End* (New York: Random House, 1954), 61.
3. Virginia Woolf, *A Room of One's Own* (New York: Harcourt Brace Jovanovich, 1963), 10–11.
4. Woolf, 17–18.
5. Woolf, 24.
6. Woolf, 38.
7. Karl Marx, "Economic and Philosophical Manuscripts—The Third Manuscript," *Early Manuscripts*, trans. and ed. T. B. Bottomore (New York: McGraw-Hill, 1963), 191.
8. Pierre Bourdieu, *Distinction* (Cambridge: Harvard University Press, 1984), 196.
9. Bourdieu, 243.
10. Theodor Adorno, *Minima Moralia* (New York: NLB/Schocken Books, 1974), 168.
11. Elaine Walster and G. William Walster, *A New Look At Love* (Reading, Pa.: Addison-Wesley, 1978), 136–138.
12. James Atlas, "The Changing World of New York Intellectuals," *New York Times Magazine*, August 25, 1985, 71.
13. Carol Stack, *All Our Kin* (New York: Harper & Row, 1975).
14. Viviana Zelizer, "The Social Meaning of Money: 'Special Monies,' " *American Sociological Review* 95 (1989): 342–377.

Chapter 5
Money and Loss

1. Ned Rorem, *An Absolute Gift: A New Diary* (New York: Simon and Schuster, 1978), 246.

2. Jose Yglesias, *The Goodbye Land* (New York: Pantheon, 1970).

3. Joan Gould, "Hers," in *Hers—Through Women's Eyes: from "Hers" Column of the New York Times*, ed. Nancy R. Newhouse (New York: Harper & Row, 1986), 286.

4. Sigmund Freud, "A Special Type of Choice of Object Made by Men" [1910], in *Collected Papers of Sigmund Freud* (New York: Basic Books, 1959), IV, 192–216.

5. Philip Slater, *The Pursuit of Loneliness* (Boston: Beacon Press, 1970), 96.

6. Rene Girard, *Deceit, Desire, and the Novel: Self and Other in Literary Structure* (Baltimore: Johns Hopkins University Press, 1966), 68–70.

7. Evelyn Waugh, *Brideshead Revisited* (New York: Dell, 1960), 46.

8. Waugh, 156.

9. Waugh, 207.

Chapter 6
Lesser Trumps

1. Michael Lewis, *Liar's Poker* (New York: Norton, 1989), 168–169.

2. Lewis, 201.

3. Lewis, 59–60.

4. Lewis, 34.

5. Donald Trump, *Trump: The Art of the Deal* (New York: Random House, 1987), 1.

6. Zick Rubin, "Keeping Count," *New York Times Magazine*, November 3, 1985, 80.

7. Maureen Orth, "What's Love Got to Do With It?" *Vanity Fair*, August 1990, 129.

8. Viviana Zelizer, "The Social Meaning of Money: 'Special Monies,' " *American Journal of Sociology* 95, (1989): 342–377.

9. Jane Bryant Quinn, "A Marriage in Financial and Other Trouble," *San Francisco Chronicle*, July 2 1988, B2.

Chapter 7
Spenders and Payers

1. Philip Blumstein and Pepper Schwartz, *American Couples: Money, Work, and Sex* (New York: William Morrow, 1983), 55.

2. William Kaufmann, "Some Emotional Uses of Money," in *The Psychoanalysis of Money*, ed. Ernest Borneman (New York: Urizen Books, 1976), 237–238.

Chapter 8
Parents and Children

1. Janet Malcolm, *Psychoanalysis: The Impossible Profession* (New York: Knopf, 1981), 6.
2. Allen Wheelis, *On Not Knowing How to Live* (New York: Harper Colophon, 1976), 112.

Chapter 9
What Price Justice?

1. Theodor Adorno, *Minima Moralia* (New York: NLB/Schocken Books, 1974), 32.

Chapter 10
The Work of Love

1. Friedrich Nietzsche, *The Gay Science*, quoted in Simone de Beauvoir, *The Second Sex* (New York: Vintage, 1974), 713.
2. de Beauvoir, 713–714.
3. Arlie Hochschild, *The Managed Heart* (Berkeley: University of California Press, 1983), 164.
4. Hochschild, 165.
5. Christopher Lasch, *Haven in a Heartless World: The Family Besieged* (New York: Basic Books, 1977), 5.
6. John Ruskin, "Of Queens Garden," quoted in Kate Millet, *Sexual Politics* (New York: Avon, 1970), 98.
7. Judy Auerbach, Linda Blum, Vicki Smith, and Christine Williams, "On Gilligan's In A Different Voice," *Feminist Studies* 11, 1 (Spring 1985): 149–161. For an example of this kind of thinking, also see Dorothy Dinnerstein, *The Mermaid and the Minotaur* (New York: Harper & Row, 1976).
8. Elizabeth Janeway, *Powers of the Weak* (New York: Morrow, 1981), 158.
9. Christopher Lasch, *Haven in a Heartless World*, cited above, and *The Culture of Narcissism: American Life in an Age of Diminishing Expectations* (New York: Norton, 1979).
10. *Haven in a Heartless World*, xvi–xvii.
11. Barrie Thorne, "Feminist Rethinking of The Family: An Overview, in *Rethinking The Family: Some Feminist Questions*, ed. Barrie Thorne with Marilyn Yalom (New York: Longman, 1982, 12–13).
12. Thorne, 15.

13. Thorne, 5.

14. Jane Collier, Michelle Z. Rosaldo, and Sylvia Yanagisako, "Is There a Family? New Anthropological Views," in Thorne and Yalom, 34.

15. Collier et al., 35.

16. Barbara Ehrenreich, *The Hearts of Men: American Dreams and the Flight from Commitment* (Garden City, N.Y.: Doubleday Anchor, 1984), 12.

17. Ehrenreich, 11.

18. Ann Swidler, "Love and Adulthood in American Culture," in *Themes of Work and Love in Adulthood,* ed. Neil Smelser and Erik Erikson (Cambridge: Harvard University, 1981), 129–130.

19. Swidler, 134–135.

20. Swidler, 135.

21. Swidler, 135.

22. Wendy Kaminer, "The Divorce Industry" *7 Days*, February 22, 1989, 30.

23. Claudia H. Deutsch, "Prenuptial Decrees Up, Prenuptial Trust Down," *New York Times*, November 19, 1986, C1.

Chapter 11
Investing in Children

1. Viviana A. Zelizer, *Pricing the Priceless Child: The Changing Social Value of Children* (New York: Basic Books, 1985).

2. Dirk Johnson, "Boy Misses Couple Who Dumped Him," *New York Times*, reprinted in *San Francisco Chronicle*, April 23, 1990, A4.

3. Johnson, A4.

4. Zelizer, 160–161.

5. Zelizer, 159.

6. Elliot Liebow, *Tally's Corner: a Study of Negro Streetcorner Men* (Boston: Little, Brown, 1967), 71.

7. Jonathan Rauch, "Kids as Capital," *Atlantic Monthly*, August 1989, 264:56–61.

8. Rauch, 159.

Chapter 12
Squaring the Family Circle

1. My discussion of this trend in marital law is based on the analysis of Marjorie Shultz, "Contractual Ordering of Marriage: A New Model for State Policy," *California Law Review* 70, 2 (1982).

2. See Lenore Weitzman, *The Divorce Revolution: The Unexpected Social and Economic Consequences for Women and Children in America* (New York: Free Press, 1985). Also see *New York Times*, August 5, 1985, B5.

3. Weitzman, 29.

4. Weitzman, 329.

5. Judith Wallerstein and Joan Kelley, *Surviving the Breakup: How Children and Parents Cope with Divorce* (New York: Basic Books, 1980), 231.

6. Susan Westenberg Prager, "Shifting Perspectives on Marital Property Law," in *Rethinking the Family: Some Feminist Questions*, ed. Barrie Thorne with Marilyn Yalom (New York: Longman, 1982), 111–130.

7. Philip Blumstein and Pepper Schwartz, *American Couples* (New York: Morrow, 1983).

8. Rosanna Hertz, *More Equal Than Others* (Berkeley: University of California Press, 1986).

9. Hertz.

10. Stanley Cavell, *Pursuits of Happiness* (Cambridge: Harvard University Press, 1981).

11. Claudia H. Deutsch, "Prenuptial Decrees Up, Prenuptial Trust Down," *New York Times*, November 19, 1986, C16.

12. Wendy Kaminer, "The Divorce Industry," *7 Days*, February 22, 1989, 30.

13. Shultz, 274–275.

14. Kate Simon, *Bronx Primitive: Portraits in a Childhood* (New York: Viking, 1982), 173.

Bibliography

Adorno, Theodor. *Minima Moralia*. New York: NLB/Schocken Books, 1974.

Atlas, James. "The Changing World of New York Intellectuals." *New York Times Magazine*, August 25, 1980.

Blumstein, Philip, and Pepper Schwartz. *American Couples: Money, Work, and Sex*. New York: William Morrow, 1983.

Boulding, Kenneth. *A Preface to Grants Economics: The Economy of Love and Fear*. New York: Praeger, 1981.

Bourdieu, Pierre. *Distinction*. Cambridge: Harvard University Press, 1984.

Cavell, Stanley. *Pursuits of Happiness: The Hollywood Comedy of Remarriage*. Cambridge: Harvard University Press, 1981.

Deutsch, Claudia H. "Prenuptial Decrees Up, Prenuptial Trust Down." *New York Times*, November 19, 1986, C1.

Ehrenreich, Barbara. *The Hearts of Men: American Dreams and the Flight From Commitment*. New York: Doubleday Anchor, 1984.

Forster, E. M. *Howard's End*. New York: Random House, 1954.

Freud, Sigmund. "A Special Type of Choice of Object Made by Men" [1910], *Collected Papers of Sigmund Freud*. New York: Basic Books, 1959, 4, 192–216.

Girard, Rene. *Deceit, Desire, and the Novel: Self and Other in Literary Structure*. Baltimore: Johns Hopkins University Press, 1966.

Glastris, Paul, et al. "Baby Boomers Hit the Inheritance Jackpot." *U.S. News and World Report*, May 7, 1990, 27–36.

Goleman, Daniel. "For Each Sibling, There Appears to be a Different Family." *New York Times*, July 26, 1987, C13.

Gould, Joan. "Hers." In Nancy Newhouse, ed., *Hers—Through Women's*

eyes: From "Hers" Column of the New York Times. New York: Harper &
Row, 1986.

Hertz, Rosanna. *More Equal Than Others.* Berkeley: University of California Press, 1986.

Hochschild, Arlie. *The Managed Heart.* Berkeley: University of California
Press, 1983.

Johnson, Dirk. "Boy Misses Couple Who Dumped Him." *New York Times.*
Reprinted in *San Francisco Chronicle,* April 23, 1990, A4.

Kaminer, Wendy. "The Divorce Industry." *7 Days,* February 22, 1989.

Kaufmann, William. "Some Emotional Uses of Money." In Ernest Borneman, ed., *The Psychoanalysis of Money.* New York: Urizen Books,
1976.

Lasch, Christopher. *Haven in a Heartless World: The Family Besieged.* New
York: Basic Books, 1977.

———. *The Culture of Narcissism.* New York: Norton, 1979.

Lewis, Michael. *Liar's Poker.* New York: Norton, 1980.

Liebow, Eliot. *Tally's Corner: A Study of Negro Streetcorner Men.* Boston:
Little, Brown, 1967.

Malcolm, Janet. *Psychoanalysis: The Impossible Profession.* New York:
Knopf, 1981.

Marx, Karl. *Early Writings.* Translated and edited by T. B. Bottomore.
New York: McGraw-Hill, 1963.

Miller, Arthur. "The Price," in *The Portable Arthur Miller.* New York:
Viking, 1971, 343–444.

Millet, Kate. *Sexual Politics.* New York: Avon, 1970.

Orth, Maureen. "What's Love Got To Do With It?" *Vanity Fair* 53, August
1990, 126–129.

Prager, Susan Westenberg. "Shifting Perspectives on Marital Property
Law." In Barrie Thorne with Marilyn Yalom, eds., *Rethinking the Family: Some Feminist Questions.* New York: Longman, 1982, 111–130.

Quinn, Jane Bryant. "A Marriage in Financial and Other Trouble." *San
Francisco Chronicle,* July 2, 1988, B2.

Rauch, Jonathan. "Kids As Capital." *Atlantic Monthly,* August 1989,
264:56–61.

Ravo, Nick. "A Windfall Nears in Inheritances from the Richest Generation." *New York Times,* July 22, 1990, E4.

Rich, Adrienne. "Split At the Root." In Ursula Owen, ed., *Fathers: Reflections by Daughters,* New York: Pantheon, 1983.

Rorem, Ned. *An Absolute Gift: A New Diary.* New York: Simon and
Schuster, 1978.

Rubin, Zick. "Keeping Count." *New York Times Magazine*, November 3, 1985, 80.

Russo, Francine. "Live-in Divorce: Tortured Couples Who Have to Stay Together." *New York* 23, 5, February 5, 1990, 40–46.

Shultz, Marjorie. "Contractual Ordering of Marriage: A New Model for State Policy." *California Law Review* 70 (1982): 207–334.

Simmel, Georg. *The Philosophy of Money*. Translated by Tom Bottomore and David Frisby. London: Routledge and Kegan Paul, 1978.

Simon, Kate. *Bronx Primitive: Portraits in a Childhood*. New York: Viking, 1982.

Slater, Philip. *The Pursuit of Loneliness*. Boston: Beacon, 1970.

Stack, Carol. *All Our Kin*. New York: Harper & Row, 1975.

Swidler, Ann. "Love and Adulthood in American Culture." In Neil Smelser and Erik Erikson, eds., *Themes of Work and Love in Adulthood*. Cambridge: Harvard University, 1981, 120–147.

Thorne, Barrie, with Marilyn Yalom. *Rethinking the Family: Some Feminist Questions*. New York: Longman, 1982.

Trilling, Lionel. *The Liberal Imagination*. New York: Doubleday, 1953.

Trump, Donald. *The Art of the Deal*. New York: Random House, 1987.

Wallerstein, Judith, and Joan Kelley. *Surviving the Breakup: How Children and Parents Cope with Divorce*. New York: Basic Books, 1980.

Walster, Elaine, and G. William Walster. *A New Look at Love*. Reading, Pa.: Addison-Wesley, 1978.

Waugh, Evelyn. *Brideshead Revisited*. New York: Dell, 1960.

Weitzman, Lenore. *The Divorce Revolution: The Unexpected Social and Economic Consequences for Women and Children in America*. New York: Free Press, 1985.

Wheelis, Allen. *On Not Knowing How To Live*. New York: Harper Colphon, 1976.

Woolf, Virginia. *A Room of One's Own*. New York: Harcourt Brace Jovanovich, 1963.

Yglesias, Jose. *The Goodbye Land*. New York: Pantheon, 1970.

Zelizer, Viviana. *Pricing the Priceless Child: The Changing Social Value of Children*. New York: Basic Books, 1985.

———. "The Social Meaning of Money: Special Monies." *American Journal of Sociology* 95 (1989):342–377.

———. "Special Monies:Gift Monies." Paper presented at the annual meeting of the American Sociological Association, August 1989.

Index